THE POWER OF GREEN

The Ripple Effect of Every Dollar You Spend

THE POWER OF GREEN

The Ripple Effect of Every Dollar You Spend

AMY O'BRIEN

Niche Pressworks

Indianapolis

THE POWER OF GREEN

ISBN: 978-1-946533-79-1 E Book

978-1-946533-78-4 Paperback

©2020 by Amy O'Brien

For permission to reprint portions of this content or to inquire about bulk purchases for promotional, educational, or business use, contact **thepowerofgreen@byamyo.com**

Published by Niche Pressworks

NichePressworks.com

Indianapolis, IN

DEDICATION

This book is dedicated to everyone out there who is already practicing discernment in their daily habits, especially in the way they direct their dollars, in order to make a positive impact in the world. Thank you for the example you have set and for the difference you have made. This book is also for those who are just starting out on the path with a willingness to learn and to be open to making positive changes for a better future. The world needs you.

ACKNOWLEDGMENTS

Thank you, Mom and Dad, for being shining examples of decent, hard-working, kind, caring, ethical and honorable people. You encouraged me to live with curiosity, and to view people and the world with an open mind. We didn't always make it easy on each other; but the good stuff worked its way through, and the appreciation is there in buckets. Even though you are no longer present in this life, I feel your presence. It lives within me. You've left a good mark on this world. My goal is to do the same.

Special mention to contributing editor, Abby Lodmer, whose amazing skills brought this book to life. You've contributed to my learning and growing in so many ways. Somehow God put you in my path, knowing your spirit and bright light would help lift me up to another level. You are an angel.

Many thanks to Nancy and Cecilia for always helping and listening to my endless bookwork talk; Kitty for your patience and understanding; Bob and Michelle for sharing in my enthusiasm; Ingrid and Melissa for your ongoing support and allowing me to share your stories.

To all of my friends and family – thank you for your encouragement, listening, advice, support and faith!

Finally, to my amazing and wonderful sons, Michael and Tim. Thank you for listening and keeping an open mind with all of the nutritional and health advice, (seemingly odd concepts) and information I've shared over the years. It comes straight from my heart. You will always live there within me. I love you more than you'll ever know.

CONTENTS

Dedication v

Acknowledgements vii

My Journey and My Why xi

Icebergs and Butterflies 1

Chapter 1: I'm Not Buyin' It 7

    Oh, the Clutter 8

    Life Cycle of a Product 12

    The Gift Giver 14

Chapter 2: The Shades We Wear 19

    Fast Fashion 21

    How Can Clothing Be So Cheap? 22

    Thoughtful Purchases 23

Chapter 3: Let's Talk Trash 27

    Plastics Don't Go Away 30

    How Is This Stuff Made? 32

Chapter 4: Nutrition is the Mission 39

    Food Is Big Business 41

    High Protein – Is This Really the Way? 44

    Food Oligopoly? 48

    Agua Por Favor – Just Not Bottled Please 52

Chapter 5: Killer Cocktail Anyone? 57

    Our Fate with Glyphosate 58

    Voice-Vote with Your Power 63

    Dead Zone 64

    Green Chemistry 67

Chapter 6: Left to Our Own Devices 73

    EM ef'd Up 74

    5G—I Feel the Need for Speed 78

Chapter 7: Healthcare Be Aware 83

    The Real Cost of Our Healthcare 87

    Medical Mishaps 90

    Be Your Own Advocate 94

Chapter 8: The Beautiful Power of Giving 97

    Secret Squirrel Giving 98

    Power of Education 100

    Philanthropy – A Family Affair 102

    Teach to Transform 104

Chapter 9: Our Planet. Our Home. 107

    How Land Life Can Be Restored 108

    Blue Zones 114

In Closing 119

MY JOURNEY AND MY WHY

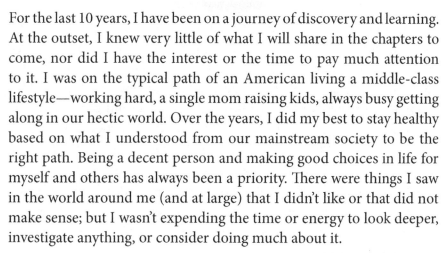

For the last 10 years, I have been on a journey of discovery and learning. At the outset, I knew very little of what I will share in the chapters to come, nor did I have the interest or the time to pay much attention to it. I was on the typical path of an American living a middle-class lifestyle—working hard, a single mom raising kids, always busy getting along in our hectic world. Over the years, I did my best to stay healthy based on what I understood from our mainstream society to be the right path. Being a decent person and making good choices in life for myself and others has always been a priority. There were things I saw in the world around me (and at large) that I didn't like or that did not make sense; but I wasn't expending the time or energy to look deeper, investigate anything, or consider doing much about it.

I had some health issues that doctors along the way misdiagnosed or dismissed. I learned to live with them. There seemed to be no other choice… until one day, something sparked me to do a little research. This gradually opened up a whole unforeseen world and gave me a new, wonderful lease on life. Little did I know that the day I decided to do "a little research" was only the beginning.

At several points during the process of discovery surrounding my health, I uncovered things in other areas of life. I felt like my blinders were being lifted. Over time, it began to occur to me that it was my relationship with (and understanding of) the power of money and related consumer decisions that needed realignment in order to leave a footprint that I could be proud of.

As time went on, there were elements I noticed and started to question in the areas of food, health, medical practices, the products marketed to us, and beyond. So much of what I learned was confusing and frustrating. Some of the information and messages presented to us as consumers seemed completely illogical and counterproductive. I began asking questions and looking behind the scenes. As I started to peel back the layers, I was often astounded at what I discovered. This inevitably led to further investigation, because I didn't completely believe (or *want* to believe) what I was finding.

None of what I have put together here is a huge secret that only I have uncovered. There have been many before me who have sounded the sirens. The information is out there; though I understand that sometimes we would rather pretend that everything is rosy. There is bliss in being oblivious! It is easy to brush things aside and go on with life-as-usual. There is plenty to keep us busy without spending an endless amount of time trying to trace the path of the seemingly illogical.

My curiosity, frustration and questions along the path of greater understanding grew with each passing year, as did my motivation to do more research. Suffice it to say that my discovery and journey have reshaped my world. Ultimately, I believe that what I've learned is worthy of being passed along.

Perhaps you are now where I was ten years ago. Maybe you are further along in your discovery. Wherever you are, I hope that what lies ahead in these chapters will spark some transformative energy and inspire you to make positive changes that will benefit you, your loved ones, and- (in the bigger picture)- our world. After all, we are all on this big rock together.

ICEBERGS AND BUTTERFLIES

Everything you do matters. Every move you make and every action you take will have an effect within you and around you. *The Power of Green* takes you inside our world of spending and directing money energy and looks at the ripple effect we create with our decisions, knowingly or unknowingly.

I believe that many people are asleep at the wheel (as I was). Most give little conscious thought to what they are encouraging based on how they spend their money on a regular basis. The effect can be either positive or negative. We all want the world to be a more encouraging, enjoyable, happy and healthy place. It is up to each one of us to make that happen. How we spend our money, and how we focus our attention and direct our intentions as consumers can make a difference. I call that the *Power of Green*. We have the ability to choose how to use that power. The key is awareness.

There are billions of us who want the world to be a better place. Are we headed for self-destruction with all that we are doing to ourselves and our planet in this century, as many believe? Can the actions of one person move us all toward that better place? If you knew there was something you could do that wasn't all that difficult, would you do it?

1

How invested are you as a human-being today to make the world a better place?

It seems like society, and the issues we deal with on a regular basis have changed dramatically in just a couple of generations. Some of the changes have been for the better, no doubt. And some may *seem* better. but may not actually be. There is an illusion that *all* of these rapid changes are making our lives better. If you've had the opportunity to talk with parents and grandparents, you've probably found that they have a wealth of information and amazing stories of the past.

Take a trip back in time. Imagine that you are living one hundred years ago (at your current age). What might the world have been like then? Now imagine that you were able to travel forward through time, to today. What do you think you would notice most about the general feeling and pace of things?

Think of the amount of information that is currently coming at you from every direction. It would likely be completely overwhelming for the "you" from 100 years ago. In our world today, we live with this on a daily basis. It is silently overwhelming us. But we barely notice. This overwhelm blinds us to what is quietly happening. History can be very telling.

My grandfather was a young adult in 1912, living in New York City. He learned to be a ham radio operator and was fascinated by the technology and the ability to communicate over airwaves with people in faraway places. He took the time to learn Morse Code. It was from his curiosity and willingness to learn that he found himself one morning able to listen in on the communication from the rescue ship, the Carpathia, about the survivors from the Titanic coming into the harbor. One can only imagine the incredible shock he and others felt when they learned that the most impressive and massive ship ever built had gone down and that many lives were lost. My grandfather (years later) wrote a letter to my brother about his memories of the experience. In part of his letter he wrote:

By 12:30 AM Monday morning the Titanic operator finally raised the Carpathia, which was some sixty miles away. Several other vessels answered the call but they were all too far away. The Titanic sank at 2:18 AM. I won't go into the details of life boats and rafts. It was bitterly cold. A few minutes after 4 AM the Carpathia arrived - too late for any peope in life preservers in the water. They died from exposure.

When the Carpathia made the final count of those rescued, it was a pitiful 711 persons.

The Carpathia arrived in New York on Thursday. I was eighteen years old at the time, and not as good at copying "wireless code" as I am now. But I did hear the Carpathia some time during that day in contact with, if I remember correctly MSE at Sea Gate, not too far from where we lived, and the operator was sending the names and addresses of those on board, rescued from that terrible disaster.

Over 2,200 boarded for the voyage. More than two-thirds perished. There was so much confusion about what happened to the Titanic. The whole world was shocked. How could this happen?

Many of the passengers bought into the dream of a better world and were excited to travel to America. Others wanted to be part of the latest and greatest thing.

If the passengers knew of the danger, would they have bought the ticket or agreed to take the voyage? If their loved ones had any idea, would they have encouraged them to go? There were matters going on behind the scenes that few were aware of. There were barely enough lifeboats for half of the passengers, due to a last-minute change in the aesthetics of the ship. There was no major disaster plan. There were egos involved and a desire to break the transatlantic speed record. Perhaps the most dangerous part was the thinking that the Titanic was unsinkable and could not go down. There were a few who were concerned. There were warnings (literal and otherwise) before and during the voyage. All were ignored.

I am using the story of the Titanic to compare with the dangerous waters in our modern world that many are choosing to ignore. We have the opportunity to turn the ship around, or at the very least, to slow it down, in order to avoid some major catastrophes. But this requires some insight, adjustment of a few habits, and willingness to be unpopular at times.

We all want to be accepted and admired and not feel like we are missing out. We all want a better life in one way or another. To achieve a better life and world, we have to be willing to do something about it. I'm hoping that you will take a few suggestions from my book, which will help us all move in the right direction. If we know, feel and understand that something is not right and is leading us on the wrong path, isn't it our responsibility to do something about it or at the very least not encourage it? We are influencers in time. The time is now to make some waves, and to do whatever we are able to do to get people to wake up. We must even go against the grain on occasion, when the result will be for the greater good. There are icebergs out there. We only see the tips of them. Most of the time we choose to ignore or avoid them, and to thrust full speed ahead. We encourage our loved ones to do the same. This leaves us vulnerable and leaves no warning for others who follow in our wake.

Can we use common sense, technology and science to course-correct and not only avoid the looming icebergs, but actually steer towards better waters? Yes, we can. It all starts with little steps that each one of us can take.

Can one person really make a difference? Most alive today know of or have at least heard of the butterfly effect. It is the premise that a butterfly can flap its wings on one side of the world, setting molecules of air in motion that cause a chain reaction that eventually influences the other side of the world. It was originally presented by Edward Lorenz in a paper in 1963.[1] People thought the concept was nuts. But the story was so interesting and thought-provoking, it hung around. Some scientists theorize that the principle applies to any form of moving matter, including people.

Every day we vote with our dollars. With every vote, we send a wave out into the world. With every purchase, we send a clear message that we want more of something. We make a statement when we direct our money. We have the opportunity to vote "yes" or "no" numerous times per day in our modern lives. Some monetary votes have a minor impact. Some have a much larger impact. If you add up all the votes you've cast in a year, it is not a small wave. It is a tidal wave.

LEAN IN WITH A CURIOUS EYE

In the following chapters, we will dive into various areas, such as our consumer habits, our product purchases, what we wear, how we live, what we eat, our healthcare decisions, how we give and more. We will explore how all of our choices affect everything on the planet. You will learn terms that are critical to understand as part of your journey to discover the power of your green:

FAST FASHION

FOOD OLIGOPOLIES

GLYPHOSATE

THE DEAD ZONE

GREEN CHEMISTRY

BLUE ZONES

By the time you finish this book, it is my hope that you will have gained a heightened awareness and a deeper knowledge about these and other important matters going on in our world today—issues that affect and shape all of our lives.

My feeling is that most people are unaware of many of these critical matters. There are distractions in our lives; some of which may be by design to keep us from looking behind the curtain. But we must take a deeper look and start asking questions. Why does the cost of everything keep rising? Is there any end in sight? Why are illnesses increasing rather than decreasing, given that we have more supposed advances in medicine than at any other time in history? Can we trust the quality of our food and the everyday products marketed to us? We can ignore these issues, but they will not fade away.

My goal is not to convert you to any specific group or belief: It is to broaden your scope; to encourage you to ask questions when things don't make sense and to stand up for yourself and for those you care about who cannot advocate for themselves.

What do you want your footprint and your legacy to be? Do you buy into the destruction or are you part of the campaign to make things better? With every dollar we spend, we push the movement one way or the other. I challenge you to remain on the side of healing the damage as much as possible. It is an ongoing challenge for all of us, including me; but the more people who open their eyes, the better. We will all leave our mark on this earth.

Every dollar you peel off the pile, every swipe of the plastic card, every click of the mouse that adds to a cart- is the use of your power, and can literally mean life or death, happiness or misery. Join me on the journey to discover *The Power of Green* and what you can do with yours. Your health and the health of our planet depends on it.

POWER UP

At the end of each chapter, you will find a section called: "Power Up – Action Items". These are suggestions for steps you can take to use the power of your green in positive ways. You may already be implementing some, or many, of them. Keep up the good work and consider stepping it up a notch when possible.

Level One is for those just starting to make meaningful adjustments. The Higher Level gives ideas about how to step up your positive influence. Don't expect to change everything overnight. That is not reasonable. Do what you can. You will find your flow.

CHAPTER 1

I'M NOT BUYIN' IT

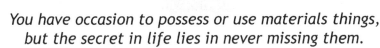

You have occasion to possess or use materials things,
but the secret in life lies in never missing them.
-MAHATMA GANDHI

I experienced my parents sell and move out of two houses—living in each for over twenty-five years. The first time, I was in my twenties and no longer living at home. So, I helped them, but I was not an integral part of the entire process. I remember thinking, "Man, they have a lot of stuff. What on earth?" But I just helped them pack and pack, and it all somehow moved and fit into their new (smaller) home.

Twenty-five years after that, my brother and I were the ones to do the final clearing of that house, when my mom and dad moved to a retirement home. My mother was dealing with dementia, which was later diagnosed as Alzheimer's, and my dad wanted to move with her. They took what they wanted with them, which was not much. For the remainder, my father instructed us to "deal with it," essentially meaning that we do whatever we wanted to clear the house of all their stuff so that it could be sold.

Well, we thought we'd seen crazy before… but there was nothing that could have prepared us for the number of trinkets, treasures and trash, or the time, energy and effort we would need to weed through everything. My caring and kind parents each had their own hobbies and interests (and apparently a bit of hoarding mentality), which manifested into an endless amount of stuff we had to sort through and make decisions about. Weeks dragged into months. It was physically, mentally and emotionally draining. I'm sure many of you have been down this road before or will be faced with it one day. God bless!

Of course, I have gone through my own moves over the years. The last was just a few years after theirs. With the overwhelming experience of my parents' home fairly fresh in my mind, I was determined to pillage, purge and whittle-down my own possessions. It took a lot of work, no doubt, but my goal was to do my best not to leave a bonkers of a circus for my kids to deal with. Michael and Tim- you can thank me later.

OH, THE CLUTTER

Think of the last time you moved. Whether it was moving from one living or workspace to another, or even moving from one car to another, I will venture to guess that you had that moment where you wondered (with cloud-caption overhead), "How did I collect so much stuff?" Our stuff and clutter is a direct sign of how we've been using our *Power of Green*, and should be a wakeup call to create some new habits for the future. Our purchase of and/or accepting of items sends messages out to people, businesses and organizations that we approve of what they are doing, and it encourages more of the same. Through my research and awakening, I came to realize that I, too, had been part of the unconscious amassing problem for a long time.

It is no secret that we live in a world of materialism and consumerism. Statistics show that the average (three person) household has 300,000 items in it.[2] That means that an average of about three people in a single household purchased and/or somehow collected over 300,000 items at various points in life, and decided to bring those things home with them. The 300,000 items only accounts for what people currently possess. I'm fairly certain my parents had this number beat. What prompts us to collect so much stuff, and what are we promoting in the world and in our lives with this ongoing practice?

Studies have shown that the average ten-year-old has over 200 toys, yet generally plays with only 12 of them.[3] We want our children to be happy and to feel loved. We assume that our children will be happier with more. That's how we feel about having so much stuff as adults, too, right? The toy industry generates over $20 billion in sales revenue in the U.S. and nearly $90 billion globally. Are children better off today with ten times more toys than they had just a couple of generations ago? What are we teaching our youth by this overloading of toys? The grooming begins at an early age.

With my own children, there was probably a half years' worth of college tuition spent on toys, much of which went toward LEGOs. Yes, full disclosure here. The excessive toys came in the form of gifts from parents, grandparents, extended family and friends. The LEGOs all ended up being donated to our church in one large toy chest. Granted, my boys played for countless hours with those fun connecting blocks, and I'm sure the kids at the church's after-school program are still playing with them today. So, while that is a good example of use and reuse, I'm not convinced that the sheer volume was necessary for the evolution of my kids—nor was the volume of money spent.

We are bombarded with ads and entertainment; from the time we wake up until the time we fall asleep. They tell us how we should live and what we should own to be happy and to feel that we have achieved success. Let's take a closer look at how this migrates into and affects our world at home.

Due to the ever-keen advertising campaigns out there, and the volume of clever marketing coming at us from all angles, we have lost some of our power to make good, intuitive decisions. At the very least, we have become a bit numb to the reality that we actually have the power to override the deluge of ongoing programming.

Perhaps nothing supports this notion better than the sheer volume of our clutter. It is everywhere in our lives. It's in our houses, garages, cars, offices and storage spaces. We find it difficult to part with our things, and we seem to feel that more is better. Our massive consumerism is damaging to our health in more ways than one.

UCLA's Center on Everyday Lives and Families did a study showing that the relationship between clutter, anxiety and stress is chemical. These feelings can promote higher than normal levels of cortisol.[4] Cortisol is great if we need to fight off a tiger, but when chronically elevated, cortisol can have detrimental effects on weight and immune function and can increase the risk of chronic disease. This gives a whole new meaning to being *weighed down* by our stuff.

Another study by Princeton University found that our reaction to clutter negatively affects our ability to focus and to process information.[5] There is an over-stimulation factor that causes our senses to work overtime. Our brain is very powerful and is constantly working for us. We process information on everything we see, smell, touch, hear and taste. Even though we walk into the same room, open the same drawer, closet, etc., with the same clutter that's been there for weeks, months, or even years, the brain has to process it every time, anew. This can make it difficult to fully relax in our own homes.

You can compare this "brain processing time" to driving a car. Have you ever had the pleasure of teaching someone to drive a car and get out on the open road with them? Now that is a startling reminder of how our minds can process dozens of bits of information at one time or rather how someone learns to.

When we see clutter, signals are sent to our brains telling us that our work is never done; signals that we don't even realize are being sent. The brain sees and processes everything in that closet or drawer or space. If messy or cluttered, it triggers a sense that we are never finished with what we are doing in the moment or that we are failing. Clutter and mess can cause feelings of guilt, embarrassment and even shame. It can also promote subconscious frustration and anger.

Now that you may want to curl up in a ball and hide (sorry), let's flip this and focus on the positive aspects of having clear and open space in our lives and how this applies to our power of green.

Open spaces allow our minds to be more creative and productive. We have better focus, thinking, brainstorming and problem-solving ability in open spaces. We feel more of a sense of accomplishment. We are better able to relax and experience peace. Can you feel your cortisol levels lowering already, just thinking about this?

DON'T WAIT

You can start the process of decluttering **right now** by committing to buying less. Make conscious buying decisions every time you shop. Bring as little as possible into your home from this point on. An important step in this is to be grateful for what you have. Most of us would be considered rich beyond wild imagination by those in our world who have next to nothing (including little education or opportunity to change their plight). Acknowledge your gratitude for everything that you have acquired. Take a deep breath, and open that first drawer.

Remind yourself to be grateful as you gaze upon the accumulated treasures. Set the negative feelings and emotions aside. Assess what you have and what you need and want to keep. Determine what will be useful for someone else and can therefore be repurposed, given away or sold. Figure out what can be recycled. Try to make throwing things away the very last option on the list—only for items that absolutely must be thrown out. Hopefully, your trash pile is smaller than the rest.

Don't wait until your next home move. There will be a lot going on then. Do what you can now to feel like you are making some progress. It doesn't have to be perfect. Congratulate yourself when one space is done. Open that nice, clear, decluttered drawer each day and absorb the good vibes. This makes it easier to keep going. AND it makes your commitment to buying less even stronger and more meaningful every day.

Enlist help from family and/or friends. The buddy system is a wonderful approach to help make the decluttering process fun and productive. It's also a great way to spend quality time with people. You can work on your own spaces and then offer to assist your loved ones in cleaning an area in their space. This keeps the positive cycle going.

There are many free videos online and amazing books that offer great advice on clearing your clutter. In addition, there are wonderful people out there who you can hire to help; because, let's face it, sometimes the task calls for a professional! The rewards will far outweigh the cost. Remember that the most important step is to BUY LESS. Imagine your living space as a safe haven for you and your family to feel better, healthier, and happier. Use the power of your green to create this in your world.

Okay, this is not a book about organizing and clearing your clutter. The purpose of that exercise is to get you thinking about how you spend your money on possessions, and about what results from those buying decisions. Does it help create what you want in your life and in the world at large? Get to the realization that more is not always better. In fact, less is generally *much* better. The *less is more* approach with regard to our consumerism, will ultimately cut down on the monetary ripple effect that encourages the production of more unneeded products and junk. The "stuff" that we somehow thought we needed ends up doing more harm than good for us in our living spaces, as well as in the environment as a whole. Continued awareness and reducing our consumerism are positive steps towards better overall health, as we will keep ourselves more mentally and physically balanced within our own homes, cars and workspaces.

LIFE CYCLE OF A PRODUCT

Let's look at this from the altitude of the full life cycle of a product. Think for a moment about the real cost.

There are multiple ways we direct our energy to buy something. Sometimes, we're shopping for one thing in particular and making an effort to find the right product at the right price. Other times, we may just pick it up or pick it out, putting it into our cart (actual or online). Before you click to check out or walk to the cashier to pay and leave, give yourself a moment to think about the following:

- What resources did it likely take to produce that item?
- Where does the profit from purchasing the item actually go?
- What resources did it likely take to ship and store that item?
- Is this something that will just add to my clutter, or will I really use it on a regular basis?
- How long am I likely to have the item?
- What will happen to it at the end of its time with me?
- What will likely happen to it at the end of its useful life, after it has been passed on from its time with me?
- What am I encouraging more of when I vote yes to this purchase?
- Does all of that align with what I want in my life and the world?

Sometimes the answer is yes. And that's great. But more often than not, if we really take a moment to use the amazing, informed, decision-making part of our brains, the answer will be no.

What we usually see when we take inventory of our stuff, is the result of past spending—with little intention and perhaps careless thought. I'm referring to a variety of things with the phrase "what we usually see." I mean the clutter and over-consumerism we see in our own lives and the trash we see in our landfills and oceans. And it's also what we see from the marketers and advertisers who understand that most of us are numb and gullible and will keep brainlessly buying and buying. There are many negative facets to this unconscious purchasing problem. I challenge you to spend with thought and intention, from this point forward.

Think of what you have actually been supporting in all of your years of spending. Now, look at how you can transform your impact and make a progressive difference with your new mindset.

THE GIFT GIVER

One cannot have a proper discussion about over-consumerism without mentioning the "gift giver." If you've ever worked in an office environment, you know the story. There's always one person who can't let a birthday go by without getting everyone to sign a card, get cake, buy birthday napkins, plates—maybe balloons, and perhaps a gift. Everyone is dragged into the conference room to celebrate and sometimes (gulp) sing. You may have a family member who goes over-the-top with every celebration and holiday. Decorations, gifts, and doodads galore are their game. They will have holiday decorations to rival the Macy's Thanksgiving Day Parade. And OMG, the ribbons and wrapping paper? Their stash is enough to supply the whole block. This person loves all of it. The more, the merrier.

Our society has perpetuated the notion that if we don't give something tangible, we are not demonstrating that we appreciate and care. Don't get me wrong, these people have hearts of gold. Some of my best friends are gift-givers. The notion here is that they may want to rethink their power of green. There are ways to show love and appreciation that don't end up in a landfill or at the bottom of the ocean and that your kids won't end up having to deal with (probably throwing away) when their gift-giver parent passes on.

It is important to try to help the gift-givers. I am quite sure they don't understand or haven't given much thought to the potential downside of their actions. Since these good-intentioned folks may do more material consuming than three or four people combined, your intervention could have a huge impact and can be very helpful for the good of all! Hopefully, they will open their eyes and consider what they are encouraging more of- like, for example, chemical production, non-biodegradable plastics, and other materials that are detrimental to life on earth, and which will end up taking up too much space in a landfill in a short time. Maybe you can help them realize that the true cost of their excessive gift-giving actions far outweighs their intentions to make people feel good. Be prepared. They will not go down without a fight. They may need a support group for their recovery. And they'll probably give you a gift as a thank-you in the end.

The gift-giver assumes that others are as excited as they are about all of the bright colored, shiny, eye-catching, plastic, metal and paper items that they love to purchase and give out. They aren't thinking about the fact that those items were probably made in a third-world country, under less-than-human-friendly conditions. And, they've likely given little to no thought to the chemical waste that results from the manufacturing of the products they've purchased, or to who truly profits from the sales. All the gift-giver sees is the end product that makes her/him smile and feel good. But not everyone shares that satisfaction—certainly not the countries whose land and waterways are decimated by the pollution on the front and back ends of careless production and consumerism.

That being said, there is nothing wrong with giving gifts to those you love, appreciate and care about. I am simply encouraging us to use some common sense, and to put the focus on purchasing items that are meaningful and useful to the recipient over a decent period of time.

BUT I HAVE TO GIVE THEM *SOMETHING*

What are some gift options that don't feed into negligent consumerism, and which can lessen the damage to our planet?

Give an experience – Tell them you'll pick them up to go for a walk, bike ride, museum visit or a yoga class. You could attend a class together, concert, go to a fun event or tour a part of your city or the

THE POWER OF GREEN

surrounding countryside (whatever they might like). Offering to spend time with people can be one of the best gifts.

Gift an educational book – Think about what they might be interested in. Audiobooks are a great choice. If you give a print book, encourage them to read it and then pass it on. You are giving them permission and encouragement to pass along their newly acquired knowledge and inspiration.

Offer your time – Offer to help them clear out a closet. If they are a gift-giver, they will have plenty to clear, I promise. Everyone has a project where they would welcome help. This can be meaningful time spent together that will always be remembered and appreciated. You can also help make sure things that aren't kept are properly distributed to the recycling, donation and trash piles. With that in mind, this process will result in you helping in a broader sense, too.

Be creative – If you have a lot of photos with friends or family, create a slideshow or other such memory book that captures the moments from a trip you took, a family gathering, or just images from over the years. These can be done with little or no cost and can be emailed if you want to avoid a printed book. This is a very special gift that will certainly be appreciated.

The tangible gift – If you do elect to give something tangible, think of the recipient and what he/she/they will like and actually use. Get to really know your recipient or ask the people who may know them better than you do, what they might like. At the point of giving, tell your recipient that it is okay to regift if so desired. Yes, there, I said it. Regifting is not a bad thing if it helps some manufactured item land in the hands of someone who will actually want and use it! Now, each case is different, and one must use good judgment, of course. We don't want to hurt feelings or be callous. The topic here is about the average gift that is given just for the sake of filling a void or because you think it will be expected. The point is to stop and think about your purchase. What are you really encouraging more of, and what message are you sending? I'm just saying- be selective and consider your recipient.

Bring it on home - Another *Power of Green* gift idea is inviting people to your home. This is a wonderful way to show appreciation. Sadly, it seems to be somewhat of a dying art. It seems many feel that it's easier to go out to a restaurant rather than to invite friends into their own homes. With so many dining-out options today, this is easy to understand, though inviting guests into to your home is a very personal gesture, and a special way to honor people. It shows a great deal of care and respect. Try not to let hosting people overwhelm you; there is no need to go overboard to the point of overwhelm. I'll tell you from experience- practice makes perfectly calm when it comes to hosting. Consider this down-home option more often than gifting people a meal at a restaurant. You can create a very healthy meal with quality food fairly easily. Again, we are trying to focus on low consumerism and the best use of your power for the good of all. People will have tremendous appreciation if you invite them into your home. That type of kindness will be remembered far longer than any trinket you could give or any night out at a restaurant. There are multiple ways to give a gift as a thank-you or to show someone you care. Think outside the usual gifting box toward the direction of what will be best for the receiver and, ultimately, for the rest of the world. Your wave of energy and thoughtfulness will be felt.

POWER UP — ACTION ITEMS

- Buy less starting now. Think of the life cycle of the product before you spend.
- Go with the 4 Rs: REDUCE, REUSE, RECYCLE, <u>REFUSE</u>.
- Minimize the "trash plastics" in gift-giving and in everything.
- Be conscious and intentional with your gifts.

HIGHER LEVEL

- Clear the clutter in your home (following the 4 Rs).
- Gift an experience, a book, or your time, or, invite them over.

CHAPTER 2

THE SHADES WE WEAR

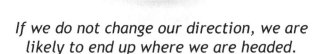

If we do not change our direction, we are likely to end up where we are headed.

- ANCIENT CHINESE PROVERB

One part of how we spend our money, which says a lot about us, is what we wear. Fashion has grown to a whole new level of excess in the past couple of decades. Marketing and advertising have us feeling that we are not cool or hip or trendy if we don't present ourselves wearing the latest styles. Have you noticed, though, that "the latest" keeps changing to a point where it's a challenge to keep up?

The average person alive today buys 60 percent more clothing than they did in the early 2000s. AND, more astonishingly, the average person keeps clothing items only *half* as long as we did back then.[6] We purchase sixty percent *more* clothing than we did less than twenty years ago? What is going on? Have you looked in your closet lately?

Most of us have closets and drawers overflowing with clothing and fashion items, yet we often complain that we have "nothing to wear," then needlessly go out and buy a new item or outfit.

Let's be real. Few of us are fashion experts (myself included). We don't really know what we're doing. It's a lot of guesswork, along with trial and error. So, we buy this or that, and it may or may not work or go with the rest of what is already packed into our closets.

Apparel can be amazing. We can feel transformed by putting on a certain piece or outfit. Clothing is an expression of who we are and how we want to be seen in the world. I believe this and have experienced it myself. Feeling good about ourselves is important, and "dressing the part" plays a role in our society, but along with that comes responsibility.

There are some hidden aspects of the clothing industry that we all need to be aware of as we use our *Power of Green* to present ourselves to the world on a daily basis.

SYNTHETIC FIBER MATERIALS

Over the last 75–100 years, the clothing industry has adopted and expanded the use of synthetic fiber materials. This has had and continues to have an enormous impact that cannot be ignored. We all wear clothes. We are all responsible. Read on.

Synthetic fibers pick up certain dyes easily, are sometimes more durable than most natural fibers, have the ability to stretch, are water and stain resistant, and can often be quickly and cheaply produced. Those are a few of their advantages. However, there are also disadvantages. The fibers are made by chemical synthesis, are not skin or health-friendly, cause allergies in many people, and are non-biodegradable (so they are around for centuries, if not forever). It is also known that synthetic fiber production results in high carbon emissions and toxic pollutants. For starters, the chemical dye waste pollutes our soil and waterways, harming humans, animals and the environment.

Some clothing manufacturers claim that cotton and natural fiber production is more resource-intensive, requiring a significant amount of water to farm the cotton, for example, or to feed/tend to wool-producing sheep, so there are pluses and minuses to each process.

FAST FASHION

Fast fashion may not be a term you're familiar with. If that's the case, today is the day you can learn about it. While writing this book, I went around asking people I knew (in addition to complete strangers, for added fun) if they had heard of fast fashion. The majority of the people respond with blank stares. They often repeated the question, "Fast fashion?" (Give it a try yourself, for educational purposes as well as entertainment value.)

Over the past few years, we have experienced a trend in the fashion industry that has tempted us to purchase more and more clothing in an almost disposable manner. There are a variety of clothing stores offering their lines at seriously low prices—prices so low, we can hardly say no. Additionally, they introduce new, trendy designs and colors on a very regular basis, promoted as what we need to wear in order to stay on trend, look cool and be up-to-date. You can often go to the same fast-fashion store every week and see a new batch of styles each time.

The clothing is not made to last, nor is the style. It is just the opposite. This is all by design. They want us to use, discard and buy again. They profit from the high and continuous volume of factory-made apparel. These items are designed to be so inexpensive that we are willing to dispose of them and come back for something new each season (or even more often). What does this direction of our money encourage and result in? In the U.S. alone, an average of 15 million tons of textile waste is produced every year.[7] This is just the waste—the actual landfill waste. And this number is growing with the fast fashion trend. Textiles is a nearly $3 trillion industry and is the second biggest polluting industry after oil. Yes, it is that big.

Nearly all clothing sold today is factory-made. Fibers are dyed (many times) and chemically treated. There is a long road of factory processes required to get from raw materials to the end product. For clothing and shoes, these processing agents can include dyes, chemicals, glues and sprays. Factories deplete natural resources in order to process these materials, which often results in emissions into the air, waste runoff into water, and disposal of potentially toxic scrap materials. All of this occurs long before items even get to the place where we can purchase them.

Recycling clothing is a minuscule practice, since it is time-consuming, cost-intensive, and since mixed fibers cannot be recycled easily (at this point). Some of the fast fashion companies offer a recycling program for your used clothing. This is essentially "greenwashing." Very little of what they take in actually stays out of a landfill.

Greenwashing[8] is a term used when organizations make marketing or advertising claims that are misleading about the environmental benefits of a product, service or company practice. These claims are made to promote a certain image to the public, and to convince consumers that their company has a higher concern for the earth or people than is really the case.

I am spending a fair amount of time on the particular topic of clothing and fashion, which I know is near and dear to the hearts of most, as dressing and adorning ourselves is one of our greatest forms of self-expression. It is important to us now and will be important in our future and for future generations to come. I'm hoping the gears are already turning, to see how you can use your *Power of Green* to be the change you want to see in the world. It can start with how you direct your money with what you wear.

HOW CAN CLOTHING BE SO CHEAP?

Bangladesh is a place that has one of the cheapest workforces in the textile industry.[9] Because of this, fast fashion companies continue to open up more factories there. They are not the only country being used for mass textile production, nor the largest, but they are a good example of another result of fast fashion purchases.

The workers in Bangladesh are paid low wages for working long shifts in poor conditions. The country also has far fewer safety and environmental regulations than many other countries, which increases human exposure to chemicals, as well as factory waste and runoff into the air, soil, and water.[10]

Getting cheap labor with minimal regulations is a dream for large clothing manufacturers, but it's a nightmare for workers and the earth. Manufacturers are making a killing, then leaving a path of destruction in their wake. The pollution created is enormous, posing a serious health crisis for the people in these underdeveloped countries, and it doesn't only affect the factory workers and local citizens. It spills over to the land, air and waterways throughout the area, and eventually reaches the oceans, where it makes its way across our planet. The toxic pollution is devastating for everyone.

The majority of textile production occurs in India and China, but the U.S. is the biggest importer of garments in the world.[11] Since the textile industry is the second largest industrial polluter of our planet, we have a greater responsibility to direct our money wisely and be a better example for the rest of the world in the fashion department.

THOUGHTFUL PURCHASES

Every time we wash a fast fashion garment, which has been cheaply made in a toxic factory- chemicals, dyes, and tiny plastic fiber particles are released into our water. Our current public water filtration systems are not designed to deal with any of that. As the water is treated, processed, and recycled back into what comes out of our faucets, many of those pollutants are coming back to us, and are also flowing out into our oceans.

After we wear out a garment, we may look at it and think, "This looks like garbage now. No one will ever want it, so I'll just throw it away." Or maybe, "It was only twelve bucks, and I wore it for six months, so, who cares?" But if that piece of clothing winds up in a landfill, it's not likely to biodegrade. Every time we purchase that top or jacket or pair of jeans for a fraction of what it would generally cost, we encourage the production of more of that throwaway clothing. Are we spending money over and over for twelve tops and eight pairs of pants when a few quality pieces could suffice and last much longer? Do you want the power of your green going towards the growth of this type of business and all its subsequent fallout?

Before you buy your next new clothing item, ask yourself:

- What will be the full cycle of the clothing I am about to purchase?
- What chemicals were used, and what are the factory production implications?
- What will the environmental impact of the packaging, shipping, and storing of the item be?
- If it's made from synthetic fibers, how often will I need to wash it, recognizing that doing so will release chemicals and tiny plastic microfibers into our waterways and oceans?
- Is the piece long-lasting and one that I will have for years, or will it wear out quickly or go out of fashion soon, ending up in a landfill? Remember that the fibers of cheap, synthetic fabric are not bio-degradable, so they will never break down- at least not in our lifetimes. They are here to stay.
- What am I truly directing my money toward? What am I encouraging with this purchase?

Clothing should never be thrown into the trash. Do some research to see what the donation options are near where you live. There are clothing recycling locations in and around major cities all across the country, and most large-scale, used-item collection companies work with a recycler to take the clothing they are unable to sell. Find one or more in your area and confirm what they do with scrap textiles. Some trash pick-up services even offer a plan to pick up used or damaged clothing, when placed next to your bins.

You'll only have to do this research one time, and then you'll have your source. Share it with your family and friends so they can follow the same practice. We all wear clothes and need to have a good discard plan. It's really not very difficult. Let's take responsibility for our fashion choices.

If you are in the corporate world or in a position where it's important that you have a current, fashionable appearance, I suggest that you consider working with an expert. Have someone come in and review everything in your closet, thin out what you are not wearing, and create a pile to sell, donate, or scrap (as described above). Share with them your interest in long-term, quality purchases that will stand the test of time and make you feel like the rock-star you are when you walk out of the house. A few key pieces can make all the difference. Consider going to consignment shops for those great finds. You'll save money and stop something from going into a landfill. Some shops specialize in designer brands. You'll be surprised at what you can find.

Don't get caught up in buying something just because it's on sale or a good price. If you love it and would be willing to pay full price for it, then it's a winner. Otherwise, it'll probably just add to the clutter, and you'll end up tossing it out down the road.

If you don't feel like your budget can handle hiring an expert, look online for some free suggestions. Better yet (or in addition), get a friend or two to help you. There's nothing like a close friend to give it to you straight- that the orange sweater does not do a thing for you and has got to go. Make a fun day or evening out of it. You can make them dinner and toss in a bottle of wine as a thank you. And you might even be able to gift some clothing items to them in the process. Win-win and progress!

Above all, stay out of the fast fashion stores. You can make thoughtful purchases with your clothing and with all your textile products—and still rock the runway.

POWER UP - ACTION ITEMS

- Do not purchase from/support fast fashion companies.
- Think carefully about all of your clothing and fashion purchases.
- Consider consignment shop purchases.
- Do not throw clothing in the trash. Find textile recycling options near you.

HIGHER LEVEL

- Do a complete review and purge of your closet.
- Donate what you aren't wearing and avoid refilling the closet.
- Use the services of a fashion consultant to find your style and choose classic key pieces that work for you and that you will wear often and feel great in.

CHAPTER 3

LET'S TALK TRASH

I alone cannot change the world, but I can cast a stone across the water to create many ripples.

- MOTHER TERESA

If you visit any average household today and need to throw something away, you'll probably need a quick lesson in how they organize their trash. This would have seemed a foreign concept just two or three decades ago. Back then, you'd go to the kitchen sink, open the cabinet door below, and find one bin for everything. Of course, we didn't have as much trash as we do today. If you've gotten this far in the book, odds are you participate in recycling to some degree. Bravo. How far do we need to go with this?

In chapter one, we covered topics about our buying habits and the lifecycle of products. One major way we can learn to use our *Power of Green* to create a better ripple effect is by looking at our trash. What are we purchasing that promotes more trash, and is one form of trash more problematic than another? What can we do about that? Plastics account for a high percentage of our consumer trash these days and are arguably one of the most troublesome waste products. Sadly, the majority of it does not end up being recycled. Then, where is it going? Landfills are one place. Another is our oceans. Neither is positive for human, animal or earth health. For now, let's take a deep dive into our oceans and see what's going on there.

One event that caused quite a stir and got people talking about issues with plastics in our oceans happened in 1990. The story of the Great Pacific Garbage Patch started when a container ship accidentally spilled over 60,000 sneakers into the ocean.[12] Captain Charles Moore (a researcher out doing his transects in the Pacific Ocean), commented that he could see plastics floating over an area twice the size of Texas. The media got wind of this and ran with it. We all believed it to mean there was something like an island of plastic out there. In fact, it was a container that fell off of a transport ship leaving thousands of Nike tennis shoes floating in the middle of the Pacific.[13] Swoosh.

NOAA, the National Oceanic and Atmospheric Administration, came up with the term, "The Great Pacific Garbage Patch." The media liked this and perpetuated the idea. If only it were that simple. If it were just one gigantic floating island of trash, it could be contained and properly dealt with. It would not be inexpensive, but it could be done. In reality, there are thousands of these large garbage patches, many of which are monstrous. The wandering trash accumulates in gyres (like a spiral or vortex). This occurs from naturally rotating ocean currents between and around the continents, as well as high and low-pressure weather patterns. Much of it is more like clouds of microplastic particles. The main term now is plastic smog, which is beyond alarming.

Plastic Smog:[14] Much like smog from air pollution that can be seen hanging in the air, we now have plastic smog in our oceans. These groupings of microplastics, (bits of plastic broken down over time from larger pieces), litter our oceans, either floating or sinking to the bottom.

Eighty percent of life on our planet is not on land. It's in the ocean.[15] Over-fishing, toxic waste dumping, and plastic dumping are slowly destroying this life source. The oceans are said to be the lungs of the earth and are certainly one of the main life support systems of our planet.[16] Our oceans provide fifty percent of the air we breathe, play a major role in climate regulation and produce many life-saving medicines, essential minerals and nutrients. Humans cannot survive long if the ocean dies.

Scientists and researchers forecast that our oceans could be dead within 30 years at the rate things are going now, because overfishing will eliminate many species, and those that remain may be killed off by toxic waste. We, as humans, rely on the ocean to survive. We *can* live and thrive, without consuming fish. We *cannot* survive, however without the essential elements that come from our oceans such as air (oxygen) and minerals.

PLASTIC IN THE OCEAN

The main problem with plastic in the ocean is that it isn't biodegradable. While sunlight will eventually break it down into smaller pieces (if it's exposed), this is an even more dangerous and hazardous scenario, because it results in microplastics that are much more difficult to clean up.

These tiny particles are in our oceans and waterways. They are mistaken for food by fish and by other organisms that fish eat. Larger fish eat the smaller fish. So, whatever plastics and toxins are consumed, tend to accumulate up the food chain. As if heavy metals in fish- (another major health concern)- weren't bad enough, we now have toxic plastics to contend with. Considering all of the pollutants in our oceans today, seafood is becoming questionable for human consumption. Essentially, our excessive waste irresponsibility is coming back around to bite us in the tail.

Ocean birdlife is experiencing catastrophe as well. In many areas, thousands of dead birds are found washed ashore, their bellies filled with microplastics.[17] They are mistaking plastic particles for food. They are feeding these poisonous particles to their babies. Their systems cannot process this man-made substance. Their bellies eventually reach a point where they cannot absorb the nutrients they need from the actual food they consume, and they die of malnutrition, organ puncturing or some other gruesome malady. Sea turtles and other sea creatures have also been found dead, filled with plastics in a similar manner. There are plenty of sad and disturbing photos of these tragedies on the internet to drive the point home. I am hoping, however, that the words here are enough to inspire us to use less plastic, and to act responsibly with what we do use.

PLASTICS DON'T GO AWAY

It is scary to think that every bit of synthetic plastic created still exists in one form or another. Let that sink in for a moment. Our small but very important part in all of this is to eliminate or dramatically reduce our usage of single-use, disposable plastic (in addition to other plastics). Let's look at this from the consumer perspective.

So many of the products produced today contain or are made entirely of plastic. This applies to just about everything you can think of. Consider the things in your home and pantry—food and beverage packaging, clothing, accessories, electronic devices, toys, household items, furniture, office items, personal care products, and so many other items we buy, use and store on a regular basis. All of these are likely to be made, at least in part, from plastics. No doubt, plastics have added incredible convenience to our world. They keep things fresh and lightweight, and can be very cost-effective. But at what overall cost?

Humans have never consumed as many goods as we currently do. A bulk of today's goods contain plastic. The production of plastics has increased at an obscene rate in just the last couple of decades. When was the last time you purchased something that was made of plastic or came in a container made of plastic? Yesterday? Today? Unless you are living on a farm or in a rural area or never leave the house (and never order anything online), odds are you are purchasing some form of plastic on an almost daily basis. Estimates are that fifty percent of plastic is used only once and then thrown away.[18] Imagine if you were required to keep all of the plastic containers you obtained with your purchases. It would probably create a mountain of plastic trash in a relatively short period of time. Where would you put it? How would you manage it? Just because we put it in the bin, and it leaves our sight, does not mean it goes away forever. It is still out there. That Thai take-out clamshell container from Tuesday night, the yogurt cup container from your snack today, the bottle of water you grabbed from the conference room—it's all still out there. And our continuous consumption just encourages more production of it.

How did we get to this point? Some of you may remember that famous scene in the movie, *The Graduate*, where the businessman is telling young Ben that the future can be summed up in one word: Plastics. That was in 1967. Oh, what a prophecy that was.

Plastic really hit the consumer scene in the 1950s, after the Second World War. Manufacturers realized it could be useful in everyday ways. In the '60s, the production of plastics increased 400 percent from the previous decade. By 1979, we were producing more plastic than steel.[19]

There were questions raised in the '70s by concerned citizens about the safety of acrylonitrile (a dangerous and illness-inducing carcinogen present in a lot of consumer plastics back then). The companies using the plastics in their products claimed that the chemical was not harmful, but in actuality, they did no research about the possible risks to human health. In fact, they downplayed any negative allegations. After being used for years in many food and beverage containers, it was finally banned.

The National Library of Medicine database describes the clinical effects:

"[Meth]acrylonitrile is moderately irritating to exposed skin and eyes. Exposed experimental animals developed vomiting, diarrhea, prostration, seizures, and coma prior to death. Cyanide is released from meth acrylonitrile after absorption."[20]

Doesn't sound too good, does it? There is more to the report, but this small excerpt gives the general picture that it's not something you want lurking in your food or drink, or that you want your family or animals exposed to. Acrylonitrile was banned in food and beverage containers *only after the public took action* (Consumer power!) There was resistance by the producers of the product, and it took great persistence on the part of concerned citizens to make something happen, but the toxin was eventually banned. A few people paid attention and realized that the chemicals in plastics posed serious health problems. They stood up and didn't stand down until a change was made. Though banning acrylonitrile was a big step, that does not mean that every ingredient in our plastics today is fine and dandy and safe. Plastics come in many forms and are made with many different chemical compounds.

HOW IS THIS STUFF MADE?

Crude oil, coal, natural gas, cellulose and chemical salt are the base products that go into the making of plastics. The most common forms of plastics that we come into contact with on a consumer level are polystyrene and bisphenol A (or BPA), in food product packaging.[21]

Some plastics are created from plants and animals, while others are synthetic, made by complex chemical processes in a factory or lab. Plastics are also processed with chemical additives for varying strength, color and texture. Just because something states that it is BPA free, for example, does not mean that it is free of harmful chemicals. The manufacturers are not even required to disclose what they use. Doesn't give one a high degree of confidence that these manufacturers have our best interests at heart, does it?

That being said, plastics have changed our world in extraordinary ways. Many plastics are flexible and are easy to make in all different shapes, sizes and colors. Many are also lightweight, insulating and waterproof. Some are strong and durable, and others are made to be thin and pliable.

They can be mass produced quickly and at a relatively low cost compared to the manufacturing of other materials. Film and music recordings are examples of how we have appreciated and relied on plastics for generations. One cannot deny that our society has grown in leaps and bounds in many positive ways due to the introduction of plastics.

The problem now is that we have so overused the blessing of plastics, that we are killing ourselves and our planet with it. Too much of a good thing? It's really time to calm the heck down with plastics. And it's time to look at what can be done with all the plastic we no longer use, need or want.

I don't believe that the plastic companies are being intentionally destructive. What we are witnessing is a common effect of our modern society's convenience-obsessed preferences, coupled with the profit-focused corporations. This combination is jeopardizing human health and the wellness of our planet, in exchange for profits and convenience. Businesses look for ways to cut down on expenses. Consumers get caught up in their busy lives and look for convenience. We are used to our lifestyles, and don't necessarily see a problem with them. Plastic is everywhere, and everyone is participating in the modern, disposable ways of living. So, what's the big deal?

We can only validate our destructive habits and turn a blind eye for so long. We need to be aware that there can be a blurred line between the regulating bodies that are supposed to protect consumers, and the companies that profit from the production of the products that we regularly use.

I'll share another example that relates to acrylonitrile. In 1977, just after Monsanto opened a new plant to expand its production of the widely used chemical, the Monsanto Research Corporation gave the EPA a conclusion that acrylonitrile pollution was *not* a serious problem. This conclusion came from research that Monsanto paid for.

Later, upon further review, an EPA expert stated that the conclusion was not reasonable, and showed proof that the chemical *was*, indeed, a major polluter. The regulators came in and another acrylonitrile ban was enacted; but only after years of some determined consumers' (and perhaps some astute insiders') continuous efforts to sound the alarm about it. We might still have acrylonitrile in the majority of our food plastics if not for these concerned people's persistence. In any case, there are many examples of situations such as this - (too many over too many years) - and acrylonitrile is not the only culprit. We need to be cautious. We must do our own research and, at very least, we need to be asking pertinent questions in order to protect ourselves and our loved ones. And by all means, use less plastic!

PLASTIC DEBRIS

Plastic debris is everywhere. If you've traveled in the last few years, visited any ocean beach, or watched the news, you've seen it. It's everywhere you go.

Many of us do our part by making sure we put our plastic containers and debris in the recycling bins. It feels like we are doing the right thing and being responsible. Even though disposing of our trash properly is admirable and is something we should all do, it is wishful thinking that doing so guarantees that all the world's trash will be magically recycled or reused.

Studies show that only around 14 percent of our trash is ever collected for recycling.[22] And very little from what is collected is actually recycled for reuse. Some recycling trash even ends up being burned (a very toxic solution). Most gets sent to landfills or is shipped off the continent, to end up polluting other countries. The rest ends up polluting the planet in other ways.

This does not mean that we should give up on recycling! Efforts are being made to improve this sad state of affairs. We are a long way from responsibly taking care of our own trash. As I just mentioned, a major amount of our waste is shamefully shipped to third world countries where it is dumped and left for people with little means and no means to fight the injustice.[23] How would we like it if the very wealthy just dumped their trash in our yard or neighborhood?

At some point, some individuals or companies will make a fortune when they come up with a solution that provides a non-toxic, sustainable way to deal with all of our trash. Interesting approaches are being tested, but not on a large enough scale to meet the need anytime soon. And there is no great push by regulators or motivation for manufacturers to do anything either (not that I am in favor of more regulations, but some incentives to cut down on the over-production of plastics and help with the cleanup wouldn't be a bad idea). Until workable solutions come along, we each need to do our part.

ONE DUTCHMAN'S SOLUTION

Hope is on the horizon with our oceans. While it has been years in the making, there are some valiant efforts being made to clean up ocean plastic. One such effort started with a young Dutchman.[24] Not too many years ago, as a young teen, Boyan Slat was vacationing with his family in Greece. While scuba diving, he observed almost more plastic than fish in the sea, and other disheartening signs of oceanic destruction. It was an experience that would change his life forever and lead him to create a major ocean clean-up effort for the world.

What started as a high school science project after that trip, burgeoned into serious research and endeavors. Slat was invited to share his ideas at a TEDx conference in 2012, where interest was sparked after his presentation, but nothing much came from it. He began his studies in Aerospace Engineering shortly thereafter, while continuing to work on his ocean cleanup project on the side. After six months, he decided to quit school so that he could focus on his mission, full time. He founded The Ocean Cleanup with 300 Euros of his own money.[25]

The following year, the TEDx video was noticed and shared by several news sites. Hundreds of thousands of people watched. Within days Slat was able to recruit a team of passionate people and raise enough money (by crowdfunding) to take The Ocean Cleanup project to the next level.

Currently, the main prototype is a large-scale, U-shaped structure that floats on top of the ocean.[26] The units are positioned in places where the large plastic gyres form and, using the ocean's natural currents, the plastics are pulled into the cleanup device. The mechanism is designed to capture, store, and deliver the trash catch from the ocean onto land, where the findings can be recycled. The technological intricacies of the machine are far beyond what I have the space to describe here. Suffice it to say, there are dozens of bright minds on the job.

Boyan Slat is now in his mid-twenties. He has critics, as all wildly creative minds testing the boundaries and norms do. These critics feel the project is a waste of time, money, and energy—that it will never work. I'm not sure what those people are doing to try to solve this major problem. Thomas Edison had 1,000 unsuccessful attempts at inventing the light bulb. I imagine Boyan Slat's critics were taking advantage of Edison's invention while spouting off.

Hopefully what he started and has been working on for the past several years will ultimately change all our lives for the better. The prospects are good, since he is not giving up. Rarely does the first attempt at anything grand-scale work perfectly the first time. One positive side-effect of the project has been bringing attention to what's going on in our seas. He has helped to create a necessary urgency about doing something before we arrive at the point of no return.

So why all this talk about plastic? The cost of consumerism cannot be discussed without considering the prevalence and impact of plastics. As you can see, the COST of our high consumerism is multi-faceted.

It drains our hard-earned money, encourages higher uses of resources, puts a strain on our health and wellness, and has the potential to damage humans, wildlife, oceans and our entire planet. No matter your political stance, we are all living on this big rock together. Let's not be selfish with our consumerism, pretending that our choices don't matter. They do. I encourage us all to take responsibility for what we are causing or encouraging more of. We have the power to shift the direction here. Let's use it.

POWER UP – ACTION ITEMS

- Avoid single-use plastics as much as possible. This may mean purchasing less or changing some habits or both.

- Use reusable drink and food containers, utensils, bags and boxes as much as possible.

- Always recycle what you can. Learn about what can/cannot be recycled, especially for items you purchase on a regular basis.

- Review the trash and recycling guidelines where you live. Each community has its own arrangement with waste management services.

HIGHER LEVEL

- Review what your office or place of business does with recycling and see if they can step it up a notch. There is more that can be recycled besides paper, generally. People often eat meals and snacks from single-use plastics as an example. Once a plan is in place and is easy for people to follow, it can become the norm.

CHAPTER 4

NUTRITION IS
THE MISSION

Let food be thy medicine and medicine be thy food.

- HIPPOCRATES

We are not only mass consumers of products, but we are also mass consumers of food. In the wake of so many dollars going towards medical expenses, it is clear that, by and large, we have health challenges. What is going on? Certainly, as previously discussed, environmental toxins play a role; but could our food choices be another prime contributor to our less than optimal health? Can we connect the dots from lack of quality food to disease? Can we use our *Power of Green* to decrease or reverse this poor health epidemic?

I am not sure when or exactly how this got lost in the human intelligence mix, but food should be consumed to nourish us, and to give us the life force energy we need to thrive. As humans, we are designed to survive on air, water and *food*. Let's start with the actual definition of food.[27]

Food: Something that nourishes, sustains, or supplies; a material consisting essentially of protein, carbohydrates and fat used in the body of an organism to sustain growth, to repair, and to furnish energy.

Our bodies have an estimated 30 plus trillion cells.[28] These cells are always in communication with one another, making sure that everything keeps functioning; though they can only communicate properly when the right nutrients are present. With poor or no communication, due to lack of proper nutrients, the cells start to misbehave. Disease is the result. It would be like leaving your neighborhood unsupervised with a bunch of teenagers and a few kegs of beer. Things are bound to go wrong.

We are supposed to use food as nourishment for growth, repair and energy. Somehow, though, we have lost sight of this fairly simple and straightforward premise. Many of us use food to soothe our emotions and suppress our stresses, rather than to feed our cells. This is all backwards. Eating food that does not nourish, (lacks nutrients and contains chemicals), contributes to emotional challenges and stress. Eating this way causes our cells to miscommunicate, resulting in all kinds of illnesses, brain malfunction and low energy levels, all of which increase the stress in life.

Where did we lose our way? Well, for starters, food industry executives buddied up with scientists and marketing experts to determine how they could manufacture and present products to get people to consistently buy more. This masterminding has expanded into the current nightmare of addictive, processed foods that we see all around us every day. They are difficult to resist when the palate is fiending for them. And that is exactly what the food manufacturers had in mind. Add addictive substances (excitotoxins) to the so-called *food* to keep us coming back for more. It's a genius business model. And they are making a killing. Pun intended.

On the opposite end of the spectrum from processed, factory-made edible substances... high-quality, nutrient-dense and chemical-free food nourishes our bodies and brains, enabling them to function properly. Real, unprocessed, food feeds us emotionally, mentally and physically. Eating healthy, whole foods diminishes cravings for chemically processed products. All of this plays a monster role in our present and future health.

FOOD IS BIG BUSINESS

Plants provide humans and animals with minerals and vitamins that are essential for brain and body health. When the plants don't have any natural medicine left in them (or very little) that's when we have a deficiency. The sad truth is, we are eating food that is lacking in medicine—natural plant medicine (phytonutrients) that we all need in order to survive and to heal on an ongoing basis from every environmental toxin trying to attack us. Our food is moving farther and farther away from nourishing our bodies. As a result, we are not thriving.

In the United States, we tend to want to do everything on a grand scale. Go big or go home. The agricultural industry in the United States is BIG business. Few and far between are the privately-owned, family farms of yesteryear. They are often overtaken or driven out by the big players. The big companies use a variety of chemicals in their high-tech, high production processes. They use insecticides for bugs, herbicides for weeds, and fungicides for fungi. These (among others) are all examples of pesticides. Toxic pesticides are sprayed on and around the food that is grown for human and animal consumption. Long-term and overapplication of pesticides have a harmful effect on the soil. It can lead to depletion of important bacteria and other microflora, which is crucial for plant and soil health, and ultimately for ours, as well.

WE ARE WHAT WE'RE EATING

Humans get their nutrients from plants. Plants get their nutrients from the soil. The soil gets its nutrients from bacteria. If the soil and plants are depleted, what does that mean for the animals and humans who eat the plants?

So much of plant growth today is executed using a toxic soup of chemicals, all in the name of mass crop production and high profits. This toxic soup includes not only all of the various pesticides, but also fertilizers used to grow the plants as large and as fast as possible, and to encourage growth on our dying land. Factory-farmed animal waste is often sprayed on crops as well. They have to get rid of it somehow, so why not spray it on the crops we all eat, under the guise of *fertilizer*? The massive amount of animal feces also makes its way into the nearby waterways. Lovely. We will cover more on that later.

We need to use our *Power of Green* to say no to these practices. This is why purchasing organic produce and products from trustworthy sources as much as possible is so important. It is important on every level, and we must vote with our dollars to make the necessary changes. Not everything labeled *organic* is going to be 100% organic, so you'll want to do your best to find reputable and authentic companies to purchase from. It takes some time to suss out and learn about the quality produce that is available near you, but it is worth the effort. Once you know where to buy the items you eat on a regular basis, you'll have made a positive change for your health, for those you love and for our planet.

As we have seen with organic farming, there are healthy, sustainable alternatives to the mass-production and highly-chemical-infused methods that are typically used to produce food in our culture. There are farmers who have been practicing better and *healthier* methods of farming for years. Of course, there was once a time, before chemicals even existed, when farmers had no choice but to use nature to manage everything. Nature is amazing and powerful. Certain bugs and animals and other plants can be a healthy part of a crop's ecosystem. Bees and worms and other creepy-crawlies are also anxious to get to work to help. Rotating crops to relieve soil has been a healthy food production practice for centuries, in addition to growing a variety of crops together, instead of monocropping. Healthy plants will be naturally resistant to diseases – just like humans.

If you have a group of friends/family who are serious about their health and wellness, you may consider starting a health-centered research group. Have each person take on a few products and practices to research. That way, the task is manageable, and you'll have built-in support. Then you can all teach each other about healthy life practices and products.

HOLD THE FRIES, PLEASE

I can't tell you the mom-guilt I now have for those drive-through trips for burgers and fries that I made when my boys were little and what I now know about the chemical garbage in that so-called *food*. Argh. Drive throughs were a quick and easy solution for a single, working mom. The food was cheap and made my boys happy in the moment. My future grandkids, however, will never have this experience with their grandmother. There are better ways to get them to a happy place and meal.

How many ingredients should be in French fries? Let's say potatoes (one would hope), oil, salt and maybe one or two others. That should be about it, right? Surprise! The most popular fast-food establishments have 15 to 20 ingredients in their fries.[29] That's not food. That's a processed concoction of substances.

One ingredient that really stood out for me was tert-butylhydroquinone (TBHQ). TBHQ is a synthetic food-grade antioxidant used to stabilize foods, fats and vegetable oils against oxidative deterioration, thus extending their storage life. In simple terms, TBHQ is a chemical used as a preservative. Its primary advantage is extending the shelf life of products. This is a chemical manufactured by a pharmaceutical company.[30]

Let that sink in for a minute.

Back when I was voluntarily purchasing and handing over this excuse for food to my own children, I never in a million years thought that I was feeding them a host of chemicals doing Lord-knows-what to their forming brains and bodies, while also encouraging the food industry to continue adding chemicals obtained from a pharmaceutical drug company.

We all realize that fast food is not healthy. But in general, I think we consumers have this notion that products labeled and portrayed as 'food' must be safe for human consumption. And we certainly don't have the thought that something as simple as fries marketed to children and gullible parents, is actually created in laboratories with a variety of chemicals specifically designed to stimulate the brain to crave more.

HIGH PROTEIN – IS THIS REALLY THE WAY?

Over the last several decades, we have become a society that consumes large quantities of meat and dairy products. This is, in part, thanks to recent high-protein diet fads. These fads, combined with the marketing campaigns of the meat and dairy industries, have caused our animal product consumption to reach an all-time high. Is this really a healthy practice? When did we get so caught up in thinking that a high-protein diet was the way to go?

The high-protein concept began in the 1960s when Dr. Maxwell Stillman introduced the Stillman Diet, which advocated a high protein, no carbohydrate, low-fat diet for fast weight loss.[31] In the 1990s, high protein plans regained popularity, and diet books promoting high protein diets began hitting bestseller lists. The money came pouring in. The Atkins Diet is probably one of the most widely recognized high protein diet programs, but dozens more are available and continue to be released today. The plans generally encourage high protein diets for weight loss and bodybuilding. Who doesn't want a well-toned, strong body?

Dr. Atkins died at age 72 due to complications from a head injury after a fall. His wife refused to allow an autopsy (possibly for religious reasons), but the New York medical examiner's office later released that Atkins had a history of heart disease and hypertension. Hmmm.

The book, The China Study, by Dr. T. Colin Campbell, is recognized as one of the most comprehensive books ever published on nutritional science and the relationship between diet and disease. Millions of copies have been sold worldwide. Among other things, Dr. Campbell's research shows a direct correlation between eating a high animal-protein diet and cancer.[32] He was raised as a farm boy in northern Virginia. His life revolved around the raising and consumption of animals and their byproducts. Later he came to understand this was the cause of so many of our health issues across the globe.

Through his studies of human health, Campbell noted that cancer was very common in certain areas of China but not in others. In 1983, he traveled from Cornell University to China with a team of researchers to study what was going on and to learn why these rates varied by geography. The team focused on approximately 130 villages with over 6,500 people. Most of these villages were located in rural China, where modern, processed foods were not available. Their findings, coupled with lab studies done back at Cornell, showed a direct correlation between cancer and consuming a high-protein diet of animal products (meat and dairy). Interestingly, there were no issues with plant proteins.

Campbell's research discovered that the hormones in the consumed animal products were part of the problem. These hormones can cause cancer cell growth to accelerate. While our bodies may periodically create potentially cancerous cells, even when we are healthy, the cancerous cells are usually dealt with without us ever realizing they were there. However, if we eat unhealthy foods that encourage cancer growth, we can get into trouble. Then, the cancerous cells will stick around. Decreasing or eliminating our consumption of animal products has been shown to be one way to lower our risk of developing cancer and other illnesses. We also don't need to support an industry that contributes to so much disease and pollution.

The biggest question then is: Where do I get my protein? An often-overlooked fact is that the animals we consume get their protein from plants. Yes. Plants have protein. By eating a well-balanced mix of quality, plant-based foods, we can get all the protein we could ever need. In the meantime, we will also be getting all of the other amazing nutrients we need in order to build our own proteins, which is what humans are built to do.

Some of the largest and strongest animals on earth get their protein (and all their nutrients) from plants. Gorillas, horses, giraffes and elephants are all herbivores. Then, the big question is, are we humans carnivores, omnivores or herbivores? We generally like to believe that we can eat whatever we want. On top of that, we've been marketed to and programmed to think we won't have much strength without meat. In reality, our bodies are more in line with herbivores than omnivores or carnivores.[33]

Carnivores and omnivores have jaws that only move up and down. Their teeth are very sharp, pointed and spaced so that they intertwine, which is perfect for tearing flesh. Their intestinal tracts are wide and short as they swallow their prey in chunks. They do not eat every day, and they do not stand or walk around much, as they need to conserve energy for the next kill.

Herbivores have jaws that move up, down *and* side to side. The majority of their teeth are flat and close together for the purpose of chewing, mulching and enzyme building prior to swallowing. Some do have canines which are mainly for intimidation or protection should the need arise. Their intestinal tract is narrow and long. They eat several times a day. They can easily stand for long periods to prepare to escape quickly should there be danger.

Omnivores have more characteristics of carnivores than herbivores. Whatever your perspective and belief, there are many additional factors which show that the human body is perfectly designed to eat, digest, survive and thrive, eating only plants. Once we arrive at this realization, the matter then becomes selecting quality, non-chemical and highly nutrient dense food. The body will perform best with optimal nutrition from high quality, chemical-free, non-processed food. This is the case for us average humans, and even holds true for athletes.

Tom Brady, arguably one of the best American football quarterbacks in history, had his chef take Dr. Campbell's course as part of his commitment to a plant-based diet. He and his wife, Gisele Bundchen (a Brazilian model), have had their family on a plant-based diet for years. This approach has worked out pretty well for Tom considering his winning Super Bowl performances for more than a decade. Many other well-known athletes and celebrities eat a predominantly plant-based diet with little or no animal products to support their athletic performance and appearance (Venus Williams, Lionel Messi, Nate Diaz and Kyrie Irving to name a few). Feel free to look up plant-based athletes to see who they are and why they made the shift. You will find some nice, well-toned and strong bodies.

By the way, Dr. T. Colin Campbell eats a plant-based diet, remains active, and takes no prescription medicine. He is 85 years young and going strong. He continues to research and lecture all over the world, sharing what he feels is important for the health of humanity. I would say that Dr. Campbell uses his *Power of Green* brilliantly.

FOOD OLIGOPOLY?

With food being one of the most important contributing factors to our health and performance, we must pay attention to where it comes from, who is producing it, and how it is produced. As a consumer, having a myriad of choices available to us is crucial for our best interest. Over the past few decades, however, something has been happening, which limits our power in this arena. Large corporations have been acquiring their competitors and other companies to gain a bigger share of the marketplace and to have more control, giving us fewer choices.

Oligopoly:[34] A market situation in which a small number of organizations or companies have control of an area of business so that others have little or no share. As a result, they can greatly influence market factors.

We've all heard of a monopoly where one entity has all of the control. Then there is a duopoly, which is a market situation of two entities. An oligopoly is essentially anything more than two.

Presently, only ten companies control almost every large food and beverage brand in the world.[35] Each of these major conglomerates own dozens of other brands that we may assume are their own entities - making their own decisions on product integrity, consumer health and safety, as well as economic fairness.

In the near future (at the rate we're moving), there will be only a handful of these huge conglomerates who control our food. This is not good, and we are not far away from that conundrum.

With oligopolies, the companies have the money to pay off lobbyists to modify laws, rules and regulations in their favor, and the consumers have fewer choices. The oligopolies also have control over their pricing, which makes it tough for small or new businesses to break into the marketplace. You'll notice that the majority of these companies (see image) produce highly processed food and/or beverage products. As a business model, their priority (naturally) is profits first. Look at your own priorities and at what you want to support.

Oligopolies in other areas where our choices are limited are in the health insurance and cell phone service industries. As consumers, we need to encourage freedom of variety, and supporting only the big names is no way to do this. Giving only a few conglomerates all of the power is rarely a good plan. Make the best decisions for yourself and for those you care about, as well as for your community. Buy local, buy fresh, look at small business options when you can. Our food/ nourishment should be one of our highest priorities. Explore and expand your consumer lens away from the big box stores that we have been programmed to direct our dollars towards.

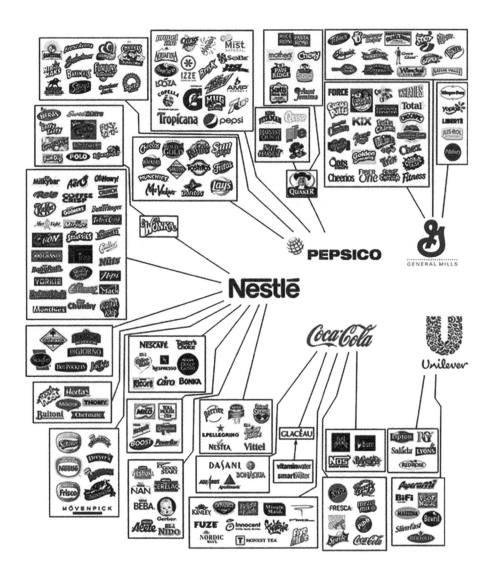

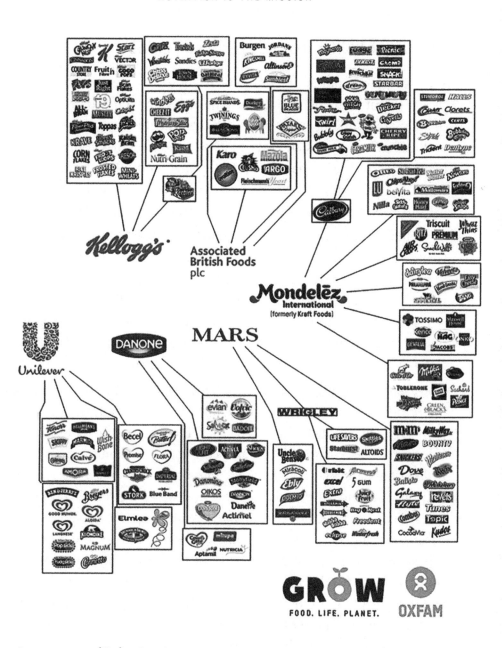

Image courtesy of Oxfam America

AGUA POR FAVOR – JUST NOT BOTTLED PLEASE

Why do people purchase and/or drink bottled water? Studies have shown that it is mainly about convenience. Many want to be healthy, so they are drinking more water throughout the day, and a plastic bottle of water is quick and easy to buy. Others feel that bottled water is healthier and safer than tap water. Spoiler alert… most of it is tap water. Let's dive into why this is one area where most of us can easily use our *Power of Green* to change things dramatically for the better.

Selling bottled water has been called "The Marketing Trick of the Century." In the U.S., we pay nearly 2,000 times more for bottled water than for tap water. That is more than we pay to fuel our cars. What's worse is that most bottled water comes from public water sources (PWS), essentially from tap water. Perrier was one of the first to get the bottled water trend going with their pretty green bottles of sparkling water. It became somewhat chic to drink, and the rest is history.

After that, it didn't take too long for the beverage companies to figure out that they could make a fortune adding bottled water to their array of products. Today, half a billion bottles are sold in the U.S. every week. That is 500,000,000 (to give a visual on the number). It takes an estimated 500 years for one bottle to biodegrade. Given that only around 10 percent of these end up being recycled, that is an estimated 450,000,000 plastic bottles ending up in a landfill, in the ocean, trashing a third-world country, or who knows where.[36] Again, this is every week. We can make a huge impact on this earth by not supporting this bottled insanity. Not supporting means not purchasing and not accepting disposable bottled water. When you accept it, you are still using your power to create a ripple effect of encouraging more. Just saying no will send the ripples in the right direction.

BUT I RECYCLE!

If this is your justification for continuing to use plastic bottled water, and therefore you feel it is okay, perhaps you'll want to consider the health risks.

Lab tests performed on a variety of brands of bottled water produced in the U.S., as well as in Canada, showed that more than half of the bottled water sold contained microplastics and other contaminants.[37] These contaminants are very small particles that the body does not recognize and can cause major health issues. PET or Polyethylene and BPA in the plastic of these bottles, for example, are shown to be endocrine disruptors.[38] These may result in estrogen issues in women, low testosterone in men, fertility issues, and a host of other health problems that occur when hormones are disrupted. Plastic, itself, can also absorb other chemicals, which are then leached into the water, and into our bodies. In truth, no one actually knows the full extent of the havoc that microplastics can wreak in our bodies. We are the lab rats of our century.

Producing plastic products also has a significant environmental impact. The plastic manufacturing process is very resource intensive. Petroleum is used to make plastic, so our oil reserves are being drained. Also, it is estimated that the water needed during production of each plastic bottle, is over one-third of the water being sold in each container. Additionally, plastic is used to wrap all of the cases, and other resources such as paper, dyes and packaging materials are needed for packaging and shipping.

The entire process consumes a *significant* amount of natural resources and energy. Tons of power is used during the manufacturing of plastic bottled water, and even more (fuel, oil, etc.) is used as the products are distributed.

When we accept bottled water, we are indirectly voting yes to all of the above. To stop voting yes to the production of bottled water, do not purchase it, accept it or consume it, unless there is a compelling or health-related reason to do so. You'll save money, the environment and your own health.

The challenge is that bottled water is everywhere—either for sale or given away. Most businesses you visit offer bottles of water. Events you attend will often provide it. When people offer you water in their homes, it is often a single-use plastic bottle. How to handle this?

When someone offers you bottled water, here are a few responses:

1. No, thank you.
2. You know, I've made a conscious decision for my health and the health of our planet to say *no* to bottled water. So, thank you, but no.
3. I read this crazy lady's book, and she told me I should say *no*.

Saying any of these with a polite smile is what we all need to practice from here forward, to tame the destruction of our own health, and that of our planet.

You can make up whatever feels right for you to say. The important part is just to not support single use plastic water bottles whenever possible. If you are in a place where bottled is the only source of water then, of course, you need to make an exception. But let's tone down the madness!

What can you do instead? There are plenty of reusable bottle options. Have one for the car and one for work. Use a good filter. It's wise to filter the water we drink in any case.

POWER UP – ACTION ITEMS

- Learn a little about what foods nourish and heal the body. Continue the learning with your loved ones. A great way to bond is in the kitchen doing something healthy and positive.

- Buy local and from smaller businesses when you can.

- Purchase and ask for organic/non-chemical whenever possible.

- Do NOT support the bottled water production insanity. Carry your own reusable water containers.

HIGHER LEVEL

- Research and purchase a good water filter for your drinking water at home and a smaller one for office and travel.

- Cut down your animal protein consumption. Discover ways to get more protein from quality plants.

- Avoid standard processed foods to cut down your chemical consumption and practices. Buy fresh, whole food and put your meals together with known ingredients. Eat a variety of in-season food and consume raw produce when possible for highest level nutrition.

CHAPTER 5

KILLER COCKTAIL ANYONE?

The best time to plant a tree was 20 years ago.
The second best time is right now.

-CHINESE PROVERB

Our food is some of the best medicine we have available to be healthy and to prevent/avoid or treat illnesses. What do we all need to be aware of regarding how our food is grown and processed and what can we do to change the course?

I remember when organic produce first arrived on the scene. It was weird and ugly looking compared to the *normal* fruit and vegetables we had been buying. It was also much more expensive. Why would I pay more for uglier food? It made no sense to me, so I rarely did. After suffering through decades of stomach pain and doing some discovery work, however, I realized maybe there was more than meets the eye when it came to the organic hype. The more I learned, the more my eyes opened. Gradually, I migrated to being on the full support side of organic... and I learned you don't have to wear socks with your sandals. You just feel a heck of a lot better. The more we all vote yes to organic, the more the prices will come down. It is up to us to use our power to change this system. If you don't want to spend the extra dollar or two, then don't buy the blueberries that day. You'll learn in this chapter why buying organic is not only the healthy thing to do; it's the right thing to do.

The brain and body health of people in our society directly relates to our social care and healthcare costs. We all pay, whether we are the ones needing the care or not. Should we just sit back and do nothing as our food is being contaminated with chemicals, our family and friends get sicker and sicker, and our government and healthcare costs skyrocket?

We need to stop supporting this faulty system *now*, by focusing the power of our green toward organic, non-toxic and non-processed foods. We can also slow down the speed of the Titanic by reducing our meat and dairy intake, to reduce the demand for mega-farming and to bring much needed relief to our soil and waterways. Be a conscious consumer. Don't vote *yes* for these unhealthy, damaging and deadly practices by purchasing the products that come from these toxic sources. As more people wake up and learn of the dangers of chemical farming, they are turning towards organic produce, and the prices of organics are coming down. Supporting organic practices and products is necessary for your health, for the health of your family, and to send the message to the food industry that we don't want chemicals in our food. If we stop sending money towards the unhealthy, mass food producers, they will notice. We can shift the tide with our dollars.

So where is my rant coming from? Let's look at what is happening to us as a result of our mass-production farming over the last few decades.

OUR FATE WITH GLYPHOSATE

Glyphosate is the active ingredient in Roundup, a popular weed killer. Initially, it was used as an industrial cleaner for boilers and pipes because it could strip minerals from the buildup within the pipes. Then, people noticed that the runoff killed every plant nearby. Monsanto got wind of it, bought the glyphosate compound, and patented it to sell as an herbicide.[39] We all need to understand what this is and what it does because glyphosate is found in a surprisingly large amount of what we eat. It is essentially poison. Yes, let's not beat around the bush.

How does it work? Glyphosate shuts down a plant's immune system, drawing out the life-giving minerals that the plant needs to survive, so then it dies. There's a problem though. In addition to killing weeds, it also kills crop plants. Monsanto decided to modify crop seeds so they would be "Roundup Ready." Essentially, organisms within the seeds were genetically modified so that the crop plants would be resistant to the weed killer. Over time, however, the weeds become resistant to Roundup. Multiple sprays are needed during each season now, in order to kill off the weeds.

These multiple sprays are in addition to the use of other pesticides. So, our food crops today are sprayed multiple times with multiple chemicals designed to kill. How can we think this has no effect on humans? If Glyphosate shuts down the plant's immune system, then how can we be confident that it won't affect ours? The sprayed chemicals grow into the roots of the plants and can remain on their surfaces.

No matter how many weeds it does or does not kill, Glyphosate has a devastating effect on the soil and on the plants harvested for consumption by animals and humans. It leaches minerals from our bodies and can kill off our good gut bacteria. Human gut health and brain health depend on bacteria.[40] We call our internal gut bacteria, plus other microscopic life-supporting organisms, the microbiome. It makes up our brain chemistry. The majority of serotonin produced in our bodies comes from the gut. This is our happy serum. Brain fungus occurs from a lack of good bacteria. The gut and brain are closely connected. The brain does not do well when gut health is compromised. It is extremely important to pay attention to what we put in our gut.

The World Health Organization (WHO) has now classified Glyphosate as a probable human carcinogen.[41] According to WHO, Glyphosate causes:

- Cancer in lab animals

- Mutation or damage to human DNA

- Higher levels of cancer in populations exposed to spraying

The warning label on Roundup clearly states that it is an environmental hazard and contaminant if it gets into a body of water. But somehow, it's okay to spray on our food?

GLYPHOSATE FOR DINNER

The majority of food crops grown on land in the United States (over 50 percent) is soy and corn. We are not "feeding the world" with our mass production farming in the United States, as is purported. These crops are grown primarily to feed livestock used for human consumption.

Since the majority of these crops are high-volume and industry-farmed using Roundup, the contaminants move through the food chain and end up on your dinner table. These mass-bred animals often become diseased, as well, due to their cramped and filthy living conditions, and also because their food (mainly corn and soy) is laden with chemicals and lacks the nutrition necessary for them to remain the least bit healthy. The soy and corn diets were not designed to make the animals healthy; instead, the animal production industry provides this food to fatten up their products and their profits. The result is very unhealthy, often diseased meat, poultry and dairy products that are sold to us through grocery stores, restaurants, fast-food chains, convenience stores, and the like.

Weeds pop up to fix the biological balance in the soil. Mother Nature knows what is needed. When our soils get out of balance, the weeds come to readjust it. They actually redistribute minerals throughout the soil over time through their root systems.

It is no wonder that these farmers have to battle with weeds all the time. The superhero greens are appearing in an attempt to heal the soil, which is damaged due to our unsavory farming practices.

We will never outsmart Mother Nature. You cannot fix a biological problem with a synthetic product. Nature will always push back and work to heal in its *own* way, which is the best way. Working with nature rather than against it, is the solution. By implementing and supporting natural farming practices, we can cut out billions of dollars in profits for the chemical companies, (which have pretty powerful lobbyists, so the positive change is not likely to happen from the top down). It will be up to us, the consumers, to change the course.

DANGERS OF ROUNDUP

Here are just three of the thousands of cases pending related to the use of Roundup.

- A San Francisco Superior Court jury, after an eight-week trial on August 10, 2018, returned a verdict in favor of groundskeeper Dewayne Lee Johnson.[42] Part of his job required spraying of Roundup weed killer throughout the schools in the district where he worked. He was awarded $289 million for his health injuries, caused by Roundup. Mr. Johnson died soon after his hearing, of complications with the non-Hodgkin's lymphoma cancer that riddled his body. Mr. Johnson is just one of several.

- Edwin Hardeman had been using Roundup on his Sonoma County property since the 1980s. He was diagnosed with non-Hodgkin's lymphoma. The jury rejected Monsanto's defense argument that Roundup is a safe product and awarded him $80 million against Monsanto.[43]

- Alva and Alberta Pilliod are another sad case between Roundup and non-Hodgkin's lymphoma.[44] In May 2019, a California jury awarded a verdict of $55 million in addition to $1 billion each in punitive damages against Monsanto.

With all of this evidence, how is it still acceptable that Roundup is being sprayed on the majority of the food that we eat and continues to flow into our waterways from all of this mega-production farming? This has been going on for years (just like what happened with the tobacco companies). The cat is out of the bag now, but the general public is still in the dark. It could be years before the large industrial farms are forced to make changes.

In all of these cases, Monsanto was unable to refute toxicology expert testimony which proved that Glyphosate penetrates the skin and disperses to the bones where lymphoma originates. You can imagine the attorney power they brought in. Money is no object for a company with a net worth over $7 billion. But real science prevailed. The evidence was just too strong.

Monsanto (now Bayer) has yet to warn consumers of the potential dangers of its extremely profitable herbicide. In 2016, The International Agency for Research on Cancer (IARC) listed Glyphosate as a probable carcinogen. Somehow the product is still being used and is for sale right now at your local hardware store, in case you're willing to risk what it might do to your family and pets at home.

More than one of Monsanto's own witnesses testified that company employees had ghostwritten scientific articles to mislead the public. They also compensated outside scientists to do the same. This gives little credence to much that they say about the safety of their products. If they had legitimate science, they wouldn't need to fabricate *anything*.

VOICE-VOTE WITH YOUR POWER

One powerful and effective action step we can take each day is to voice-vote. This is a practice where you use your voice to express likes, dislikes, concerns and preferences (or simply create awareness), whether to a store clerk, manager, friend or community member.

Sharing your stance on issues that matter will create a ripple effect without spending any money at all. Voice-voting can be used in many ways, and I encourage you to take it on. Exercising your verbal power may seem small and insignificant at first, but your voice-vote will make a difference.

Regarding the use of Glyphosate, ask questions to bring attention to this important matter. Find out if Roundup or other hazardous chemicals are used at your kids' schools, your places of work, or in neighborhood parks where you bring your kids/pets. One voice can raise awareness and will at least get the conversation started. Encourage others to do the same, and then we're on to something.

Start asking for organic food wherever you go- even when you know they don't have it. Just politely ask, "Is any of your food here organic?" or "Do you know where your food is grown, and whether or not they use chemicals?" Many small, local farms do not use chemicals, but have not been certified as 'organic,' so buying local can be just as good as buying organic.

Fifteen years ago, or so, I discovered I had issues with gluten and dairy. This was not as common as it is today. I went around for years asking for gluten-free bread or pizza crust in the Seattle area. I walked into many stores and shops knowing full well they did not offer anything gluten free (GF). "Do you have anything that's gluten free?" I would ask. "No, we don't, sorry," someone would reply. I would add, "Well, maybe you could mention to the management that people really want it." I would periodically pick up the phone and call pizza places and ask about gluten free options, again knowing full well that they didn't have any. I was simply planting some seeds- just doing my voice-vote gardening.

During this time, I used to vacation often in Mexico. In the first few years, I'd ask at restaurants if they had any GF options. They had no idea what I was talking about. Gluten free was literally a foreign concept to them. Back then, it was hard enough to explain what gluten was to people in America! Gradually, over the next few years, people began to understand my request but would still not have any GF options. Then, during one vacation, the waitperson said in response to my usual quandary, "Si! Libre de gluten," and came back with a few gluten free options. Success! Now, having gluten free options is commonplace, and many food service establishments have multiple GF options available. This story shows how you can plant a seed of eventual, effective change by asking a simple question. This is how true change occurs. When enough of us use our voice-vote to demand something, it will affect the supply.

Gluten free food is now commonly available, and many shops and restaurants offer delicious options. **In just a decade and a half, our culture went from practically zero awareness about gluten free, to a widespread willingness to accommodate this dietary need. This is the *Power of Green* using voice-voting.** People simply asking, requesting and encouraging made change happen. When people are willing to voice what they want to spend their money on, those who want to turn a profit will accommodate.

DEAD ZONE

In what other ways are toxic chemicals from food production causing issues that cannot be ignored? If you live anywhere near Louisiana, where the Mississippi River spills into the Gulf of Mexico, you are familiar with the dead zone. Once a living, thriving body of water where nearly 40 percent of all the seafood in the U.S. came from, it has now officially been labeled a dead zone. The National Oceanic and Atmospheric Administration (NOAA) started tracking the area in 1985 after concerning changes were detected.[45] This dead zone in the gulf has been growing year after year. As of this book's publication, it covers nearly 9,000 square miles.

Nancy Rabalais, a Louisiana State University scientist, ocean expert, diver and world-renowned expert on dead zones, has been researching and speaking about this major concern for three decades.[46] What is her take on the cause of this devastation? Large-scale agricultural practices. Chemicals and compounds used in the mass production of corn and soy crops and manure waste from meat and dairy farms along rivers all eventually spill into the waterways. The chemicals and waste funnel into the Mississippi, which empties into the Gulf. There is a chain reaction that results in high nitrogen and low oxygen levels in the water and living organisms die. Some fish and living creatures are able to swim out of the area. Some cannot. You could say the large-scale farming methods in the Midwest are treating the Gulf of Mexico like a toxic waste dump. And we all pay in the end.

Image courtesy of the National Parks Service

Nancy is not the only one who understands and speaks out about the dead zones in our oceans. Many are sounding the alarm, including scientists, biologists, fishermen, seafood industry groups and other concerned professionals.

What can be done? As Nancy puts it, the solution lies upstream. She states that the current level of massive corn and soybean production (mainly used to feed animals for consumption) is not going to be sustainable in the future. Our habits of eating too much meat are coming around to bite us back.

Based on what she has learned, Nancy has chosen to cut down on her consumption of animal products. She pleads with others to do the same.

The Cycle:

- Corn/soybeans are mass-produced by large-scale farming companies that use products to promote hyper-growth and high output.
- Crops harvested go to the meat and dairy industry as feed for factory-farmed cattle, chickens, turkeys and pigs.
- Animal waste floods into enormous cesspools. The waste level is exorbitantly high due to forced overfeeding.
- Runoff chemicals/compounds and animal waste gets into the riverways through ground seepage, runoff and air-spraying of waste as fertilizer.
- Main rivers from multiple states drain into the Mississippi River. Contaminated water gets carried down to the Gulf of Mexico.
- Devastation occurs in the environment, killing ocean plants, fish and organisms, creating a dead zone.

Oh, I left out one piece of the cycle. Large industrial-farming and the meat and dairy industries are trying to meet the high demand for meat and dairy products. Who wants all of these animal products? Yes, it all starts with us. The tip of the iceberg is our excessive demand for meat and dairy. The massive bulk of the iceberg lies under the surface. The environment (along with our health) is taking the hit. It is time to slow the ship down before it's too late.

GREEN CHEMISTRY

For many years now, the focus has been on creating new and exciting chemicals to aid in farming and food production. We only learned about one of these chemicals (Glyphosate), how deadly it can be, and how its manufacturers will fight tooth and nail, in unscrupulous ways, in order to keep their profits flowing. There is so much money to be made in the mega-farming and chemical industries. It will be no small task to turn things around, but we must try, for the health and safety of all.

There is definitely hope for a brighter future. Yes, Amy finally lightens up. Alternatives to the highly toxic chemicals in our world do exist. People and money are at work on sustainable solutions right now.

Green chemistry, or sustainable chemistry, focuses on creating products and processes that reduce or eliminate the production and use of hazardous substances.[47] This relates to everything grown and manufactured today. With our support, (using our power of green wisely by *not* channeling our money towards harmful, chemical products), we can change the course.

THE MAIN POINTS OF GREEN CHEMISTRY:

Prevention – Prevent waste versus having to treat or clean up after the fact.

Reduce Toxicity – Use methods/substances which will do little to no harm to people or the environment.

Design for Energy Efficiency - Minimize energy use to lessen the economic and biological impact.

Use of Renewable Substances - A raw material/organic substance should be renewable rather than depleting.

Design for Degradation – Design for products to degrade and break down at the end of their functioning life.

Real-Time Analysis for Pollution Prevention – Do the homework first to lessen/prevent the pollution later.

Safer Chemistry for Accident Prevention – Choose substances that minimize the potential for chemical accidents, including releases, explosions and fires. Keep workers and the environment safe.

You may be wondering like I do, "Why isn't green chemistry mainstream now?" Or moreover, "Why isn't green chemistry the only-stream?" I believe that the modern age started with good intentions but gave little forethought to long-term effects of their convenience-based, disposable products. By the time the negative effects of their practices started surfacing, the modern machine was in full-profit, big business mode and no one wanted to disrupt the flow.

It is up to us (millions of consumers) to send the message that we don't want unhealthy and dangerous chemicals in our food, water, air or products. Green Chemistry offers an alternative. If the money is there to create damaging chemicals, it is there to research and create healthy alternatives. This can still turn a profit for industries. Many corporations have 'gone green' and have become even more successful in the process. Use your power to push producers to move towards *greener* pastures.

JUST THE TIP OF THE ICEBERG

Of course, Glyphosate is not the only chemical we are dealing with. We breathe in toxins every day from car exhaust to chemicals in cleaning products and cosmetics. Even the synthetic fibers from our clothing leach through our skin and build up in our bodies. Hormones and antibiotics from factory-raised meat, as well as pharmaceuticals and heavy metals in our drinking water, soil and food, are nearly impossible to avoid entirely.

Our bodies carry a toxic load. Over time, this burden can result in serious health matters such as cancer, autoimmune disease, heart disease and other chronic conditions. Other signs that toxins are affecting us on a daily basis are: overwhelming stress, fatigue, weight issues, headaches, body aches, inflammation, sleep issues, brain fog and stomach issues, just to name a few. There is no telling how the combination of toxins in our world is truly affecting us. No studies have been done on the combined effects. Again, we all pay in the end, one way or another, with our health challenges. It is up to each of us to do our part and to be an example for those around us.

It's important to avoid these health-damaging poisons, but we can't eliminate them altogether. In addition to changing our consumer habits, what can we do right now to combat the toxic load? Detox.

DETOX — CLEAN-UP TIME

When you detox, you flush the harmful chemicals out of your system, helping your body to naturally dislodge and release poisons, freeing you from your toxic burden, and allowing your body to start healing.

Detox comes in many forms. There are countless products on the market designed for detoxing. Consult a professional and do your homework before jumping in. Some can be rough on the system or downright unhealthy. I've been practicing various forms of detox for many years and have had great results. There are toxins in us which can only be released when we give our bodies the space to do so. As the toxins are loosened and before they leave the body, one may experience temporary side effects like headaches, stomach aches and feeling overly tired.

These are just some of the common side effects. They will pass. It's all par for the course. Just breathe through them. Consult with a health practitioner to figure out what the best detox approach would be for you. A naturopathic doctor may be more likely to have good ideas in the detox realm. Fasting has been shown throughout the ages to be a very thorough and enlightening detoxification approach. Again, like any detox, fasting must be done *properly*. Consult a professional.

The simplest detox approach, to start, would be consuming a variety of fresh, non-chemically grown, nutrient-dense plants - mostly fruits, vegetables and herbs. Through the ongoing consumption of these foods, we will be engaged in a slow and constant detox. Plants are designed to nourish, protect and sustain us. Many will help us heal – even before something major surfaces.

We can all assume that we are carrying a toxic load, given the nature of our environment and food today. When you have the experience of feeling strong, vital, clear-minded and clean, you will understand how cleansing toxins can be miraculous, and is quite possibly the most important health move you can make for yourself.

As Hippocrates (the Father of Modern Medicine) taught us, food is some of the best medicine we have available to remain healthy and to avoid or treat illnesses. Use your power to educate yourself, make healthy choices, and change your habits for better health.

POWER UP — ACTION ITEMS

- Buy organic to avoid chemical-laden food for better health.

- Voice-Vote wherever you eat. Let's encourage organic and non-toxic options everywhere.

- Cut down on meat and dairy consumption to discourage the damage it is causing people, animals and our planet.

- Learn about and incorporate fresh, organic herbs into your meals to help the body purge heavy metals and chemicals.

HIGHER LEVEL

- Ask those in charge of grounds maintenance where your kids play (where you work, live, etc.) if they use Roundup or other chemicals, and if so, request that it be changed. Get the buzz going here.

- Incorporate one or two days a week where you eat only clean, fresh, plant-based food or juices.

- Consider consuming animal products only on rare occasions or cut them out altogether.

- Consider an annual or semi-annual detox program with the help of a professional. This is as important as getting your teeth cleaned.

CHAPTER 6

LEFT TO OUR OWN DEVICES

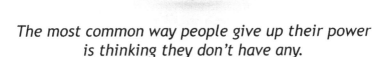

The most common way people give up their power
is thinking they don't have any.
- ALICE WALKER

Our nation has its challenges to address surrounding the chemicals in our food, which affect humans, animals and our planet. We've learned what we can do to start turning that ship around. Another way we can power up to protect our mental and physical health is by looking at the potential health hazards of our current and future technology. The first step is learning about what we don't see that goes on all around (and through) us every day.

We live in a world with amazing technologies and possibilities. Just sixty to seventy years ago (a nanosecond in the grand picture of humanity), we had telephones with cords that attached to a wall and black and white televisions. We relied on the U.S. Postal Service, telegrams and Morse code to communicate with one another. That all seems like the Dark Ages compared to today.

TECHNOLOGICAL IMPACT

Going back in time… the first color televisions were found to be radioactive. Gather 'round, family! Let's sit nice and close and see if we can glow. In 1968, after a series of testing was done, the U. S. Surgeon General issued a statement to the public to regulate the way people should watch TV.[48] Some of us may recall our parents telling us to not sit so close to the tele. The statement suggested maintaining at least a six-foot viewing distance from the front of the screen. The strength of the beam decreased the farther the distance from the screen. So, all the kids who used to sit on the carpet just a few feet from the box were getting the worst of it. Great for all those Saturday morning cartoon sessions.

The National Council on Radiation Protection downplayed the concerns, but the government recognized the hazard and established policies to protect people. The updated policies and guidelines showed that some people in high places reviewed and discussed the testing results and had concerns strong enough to enforce changes. They regulated the radiation emissions in all forms of electronics. That was over fifty years ago.

What's happening now? Surely, we can rely on our government to keep us safe, like we could in the last century, right?[49] Sadly, it seems that history may be repeating itself with the harmful inventions, but not fast enough in terms of the governmental regulations. Industries continue to take the lead by developing, releasing and selling new technologies, while the government plays catch up and tries to create safety guidelines and policies after the fact. Unlike the past, the people in high places who have the power to request more testing and to implement safety precautions aren't stepping up.

EM ef'd UP

Electromagnetic Frequencies (EMFs) are a form of radiation. Some are natural and some are human made. There are low-level EMFs that are released from microwave ovens, powerlines, cell phones and Wi-Fi, and high-level EMFs, which come from the sun and medical imaging machines.

Quantum physics tells us that everything is energy. Everything within us and everything around us is energy. The body's energy operates at a certain vibration or frequency. Since the dawn of humanity, people have been using methods of vibration, frequency, sound and pressure for healing. These healing modalities have been used and continue to be used to help alleviate both physical and mental ailments. If the body is out of sync, there is dis-ease. Certain positive vibes and frequencies can transform dis-ease into ease and health. To the contrary, there are vibes and frequencies that can be very damaging.

The sun gives life to everything living on this planet. Nature knows what it is doing. The sun is not up there shining away with any agenda working against us. We know to avoid overexposure, and we always get a break from the ball of fire when it sets each day. With human-made radiation devices, such as x-rays at the dentist or doctor's office, there are serious precautions put into place to protect us, as well as the technicians. It is undeniable that there are dangers with this high-level radiation.

The human-made, low-level radiation that is everywhere is the focus of this chapter. The radiation explosion began gradually, starting with the first power lines being erected in the early 1900s, and steadily increasing in number throughout the century, through today. Microwaves became popular in the 1970s. Then, along came cell phones and Wi-Fi in the later part of the century. Presently, just about every electronic device you can think of has a wireless feature. If we could see the waves of radiation, they would be like glowing cobwebs going all around us and through us.

So, what's the big deal? Research has shown that EMFs can affect your body's nervous system function and can cause damage to the cells.[50] The World Health Organization has stated that EMFs are a possible cause for cancer. Other symptoms may include:

- sleep issues, including insomnia
- headache
- depression
- tiredness/fatigue
- lack of concentration
- changes in memory
- dizziness
- irritability
- restlessness and anxiety
- nausea
- skin issues (pain, itching, burning, tingling)

Many instruments that surround us in our high-tech world emit EMFs. Just because it is not visible to the eye does not mean that radiation is something to be ignored or brushed aside as nonsense or insignificant. The level and volume of these damaging frequencies have increased tremendously in our lives in the last ten years. Most of us have smartphones, notebooks, laptops, wireless earbuds, and countless other Wi-Fi devices in our homes and offices; and just about any public place we enter has Wi-Fi.

Our homes are being equipped with smart meters by utility companies without our consent—or let's say they sneak it in while we are not paying attention.[51] There is not enough space to get into that here, so I encourage you to look up the information for yourself. We are being pushed to purchase smart appliances now. We are obsessed with everything wireless, and the makers of these products are only too happy to come up with more for us to obsess over. All we are shown in marketing campaigns are the marvelous benefits and the cool factor – zero about the possible health concerns.

Digital assistants for your home that rely on artificial intelligence (AI) to respond to commands and questions is another popular way we bring these waves into our homes. "Alexa, where did I put my beer?" Remember Rosie the Robot from the Jetsons? Well, that's most likely next up for the home as the AI industry is all over it. Implantable cell phones in humans are also a potential reality as early as 2024. Just say no to this wave of insanity!

We should ask ourselves if all this technology is really improving the quality of our lives and worth our being part of this giant science and biology experiment.

Some people have a greater sensitivity to EMFs than others. None of us are immune. And the disruptive frequencies affect more than just humans. They also affect our pets, our plants in our homes, as well as animals and plants on our planet. Think of how your dog or cat can feel something concerning before you do. Given their heightened senses, imagine how all these radiation waves affect them. Nervous system interference is not something that we or our pets need more of in this already highly stimulating society.

WI-FI

Wi-Fi is just about everywhere and certainly helps us stay connected. The industry is feeding on our desire to be cool, hip and up on the latest technology fad wagon, which generally includes a wireless feature. We have wireless radiation streaming at us from all angles, coursing through our brains and bodies, constantly. There is very little that we can do to get a rest from EMFs. So, even though the hits might be low and brief, if they are happening *thousands of times per day*, then one would imagine the exposure will take a toll. What are the children born in the last ten years going to experience with their brains and bodies as a result?

Children and infants are particularly sensitive to Wi-Fi radiation. Many countries are banning Wi-Fi around schools due to cognitive function concerns. France has banned Wi-Fi in nursery schools, and has put warning labels on regular schools, because they have found that there is an impaired learning capacity in children when Wi-Fi is nearby.[52] Companies are required to put up warning signs when they are installing Wi-Fi transmitters. A young child's brain absorbs 2 to 10 times more radiation than an adult's brain, from the same level of exposure.

The top four diseases that affect our young children today are brain tumors, thyroid cancer, testicular cancer and colorectal cancer. Essentially, the organs closest to where we constantly put our cell phones and other devices. We are exposing children to massive amounts of EMF microwave radiation for many hours every day during school, with no studies about the safety or long-term health effects of the waves.

5G—I FEEL THE NEED FOR SPEED

Now that we are so dependent on our devices, we are somewhat forced to keep installing, updating and upgrading to the latest versions, so that they will work efficiently. There are constant innovations in technology that keep the flow of money moving out of our pockets and into theirs. The latest buzz within the telecommunications world, (touted to be essential for keeping up with the times), which we all need to be wary of is 5G (Fifth Generation).

5G has been designed to handle many times the amount of data compared to our present network level. It uses higher frequency waves that don't travel as far, and therefore, require many more cell towers (perhaps hundreds of thousands more) that must be located closer to the ground and not too far apart to work.

In case you haven't noticed, these new 5G cell towers are popping up everywhere, bringing with them some major concerns: the frequency and high level of the pulsations, the close proximity of the stations and the closer positioning to ground where people dwell, just to name a few. Many people (doctors, biologists, politicians, concerned citizens) have spoken out about the potential dangers.

"Putting in tens of millions of 5G antennas without a single biological test of safety has to be about the stupidest idea anyone has had in the history of the world."

–Martin L. Pall, Ph.D.
Professor Emeritus of Biochemistry and Medical Sciences,
Washington State University

If you haven't heard of 5G by now, perhaps you've been living under a rock. And that could actually be a good place to protect yourself. Fifth Generation promises to introduce a new era with faster and better connectivity. That sounds good, right?

But the question remains: Are there any public health or safety implications with the installing of these multiple cell sites in nearly every neighborhood, next to schools, daycare facilities, hospitals, all businesses, and pretty much everywhere and anywhere that there are humans who want and need to access their tech devices?

What research has been done, where has it been published, and what results have been compiled? In February 2019, there was a Senate Commerce hearing in Washington, DC, to pose a similar question: What studies have been done or are being done on the safety of 5G in the cellular world? The panel of representatives from the FTC, FCC, FDA, and other communications agencies sat across from the Senators at the hearing, waiting to be questioned.[53]

Senator Blumenthal read from a clip he took from the FDA's website, which stated that the FDA is essentially leaving it up to the cell phone industry to take steps, including doing its own research, to look at the possible biological effects of 5G. Really? Isn't this like asking the fox to guard the henhouse? What motivation does the cell phone industry have to do anything, much less conduct any research that might expose their radiation towers as being detrimental to all life on earth? If the cell phone industry does the research and finds what they likely know they will find, then they will later (surely during class action lawsuits) have to admit to previously having had that information. As a business practice, that's not a good idea. So, they just try to keep things under the radar and promote how wonderful and superior their new systems are, without conducting any research that might incriminate them or their products.

The Senator states, "I believe the American people deserve to know what the health effects [of 5G] are." He then asked the panel directly, "How much money has the industry committed in support of independent research?" He stressed the word independent. "Has that research been ongoing? Has anything been completed? Where can consumers look for it? And we are talking about research on the biological effects of this technology." After some throat-clearing and filler-talk from the communications executives and experts, the answers came back that there is no money (zero) going towards any safety studies, and there are no active studies in the works.

Billions of our consumer dollars go to giant communications companies, and even more than that of our collective tax dollars go to fund some of the largest federal communications and safety agencies in the U.S. government, and *nothing* is being done to see if what is about to blanket our entire country is safe at all. The Senator finished his time at the hearing with this rhetorical statement, "So we are kind of flying blind here as far as health and safety are concerned."

President Clinton signed the Telecommunications Act of 1996 (TCA) into law. Section 704 states that no health or environmental concern can interfere with the placement of telecom equipment. He gave the power to the FCC with no regard for human health. They are not a health or medical agency. They have no biomedical people on their team—only engineers. Chew on that information.

THE SOLUTION

From televisions to wireless capabilities, technology changes how we live and interact with the environment around us. It can make many things easier for sure, but we need to be mindful as to how technological changes can negatively impact our lives and the environment.

Wireless is not the only option. Fiber optics were the wave of the future at one point.[54] They are still used but have been overshadowed and practically wiped off the map by wireless everything. If we have any chance, we need to encourage alternative approaches to the use of wireless and push for industry science studies of 5G safety.

Is all of this convenience worth it? Are we so helpless that we cannot turn off our own lights or make a list of what we need from the store? If there is a health concern, isn't it better to err on the side of caution? Do we want our children growing up in a world where they become reliant on voice commanding everything? Our countertop robots seem innocent enough, and many people love the convenience and now can't imagine living without them. There are also privacy matters at play here. Can the courts subpoena recordings in your home? Is there a risk of hacking? Can they be set to record? Who has the rights to the recordings? Imagine the value of these recordings. What people or companies would be willing to pay for this data? Do we want to live in a fully automated world? How long will it be before we have no choice? Think carefully before inviting all of these "smart" devices into your home.

For your health and the health of your family, cut down on the number of wireless devices in your home, and lessen your everyday usage as much as you reasonably can. Vote (voice, money, actions) against the deluge of wireless everything whenever reasonably possible. Let's slow down the ship and reassess our course.

POWER UP — ACTION ITEMS

- Refuse as many Wi-Fi products and home appliances (and products that will have antenna included) as you can. Smart products should be avoided whenever possible.

- Put up a sign on your current meter to refuse an upgraded smart meter, if at all possible.

- Invest in EMF harmonizers for your phones and other wireless devices to reduce the effects.

- Spend time out in nature (with your phone off or left at home). Breathe, relax, and enjoy the peace.

HIGHER LEVEL

- Purchase an EMF radiation detection device to measure strong areas in your home.

- Look up video interviews with Barry Trower, Royal Navy microwave weapons expert.

- Write to your government representatives on the state and federal levels to sound the alarm about 5G and request additional safety studies.

CHAPTER 7

HEALTHCARE BE AWARE

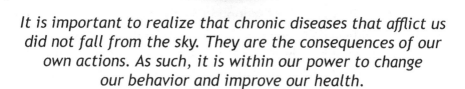

It is important to realize that chronic diseases that afflict us did not fall from the sky. They are the consequences of our own actions. As such, it is within our power to change our behavior and improve our health.

- DR. MILTON MILLS

Taking charge by using our money and voices to vote against chemicals in our food and waterways, as well as to reduce radiation exposure and encourage the study of health concerns, are positive ways to use our power, as we just covered. Let's step through the next doorway here to the healthcare industry and learn how to be a more informed consumer. In this section, *The Power of Green* relates to advocating for your own well-being and learning to keep your mind and eyes open for true healthcare within this modern-day (and sometimes questionable) system. Given that our health is the most important asset we have, we are wise to pay attention and use our power to protect it.

When most of us think of healthcare, the doctor/patient relationship immediately comes to mind. We want to know that our doctors are competent and unbiased, and that they are making decisions based on evidence and actual science—not on what some special interest group or which high-profit institution pays them the most. We hope that our doctors focus primarily on prevention, and then on providing care that improves our health. That may mean considering alternative options that are simple, easy, and inexpensive, in conjunction with or in place of prescribing medications or ordering tests or procedures.

There was a time when doctors would prescribe rest, extra fluids, even a cold compress before prescribing medication. However, in the last few decades, medical care has shifted to a more prescription-focused approach. Think about it. When was the last time your doctor suggested trying an at-home treatment that didn't involve medication? Why can't we tell them that we are stewarding our own health, and ask them if they have any suggestions for that?

The majority of medical schooling in the U.S. is heavily funded by pharmaceutical companies.[55] Therefore, the focus is on diagnosing and prescribing. It has always amazed me that doctors spend no time asking what we eat or anything about our lifestyles. Doctors are taught very little about nutrition in their medical education and training. You would think that at least a month (within that 8-12-year timeframe) would be focused on how nutrition affects the human bodies that they will be treating. Shockingly though, I have been told by many doctors only one or two days are dedicated to discussing anything about nutrition, during their many years of schooling. Does it make sense to anyone that the actual fuel for our bodies and brains is not a major area of study for physicians who are taking an oath to protect and encourage our health and wellness?

There are many well-meaning doctors out there. They entered the medical profession for the right reasons. They want to help heal the sick and improve the health of their patients. They also want to have lucrative careers, and there is nothing wrong with that. But in the health and medical industry, profits should always come *after* patient safety and quality care.

JIM'S STORY

An active senior in his late 80's, Jim loved to walk every day and take in the sights and smells of the surrounding trees that he had come to know and love from his early days in forestry in his twenties. He was fully functioning (brain and body), living in a retirement community where he was probably the most able-bodied and active of all.

Occasionally he would experience unusual dizziness or stomach pain. His daughter took him to all of his doctor appointments. She wanted to be with him to hear what was going on and to be of support. Jim's doctors ordered several tests over the years, but no issue was ever detected; so, experimenting with different prescription medications to deal with his symptoms was the expert suggestion.

Late one night, Jim's daughter was awakened by a call informing her that 9-1-1 was called and medics were on their way to her father. They rushed him to the ER. They were sure it was heart related. Exams and preliminary tests were performed, but again nothing was determined. Over the next three days, he was put through a barrage of CT scans, MRIs, EKG monitoring, lab work and just about every other major test they could come up with—all attempting to see what was going on with his heart. And what was the result of all of it? Nothing. Nothing at all was determined.

During his stay, Jim did not feel well-treated. He reported that the doctor would come in for very brief visits, was gruff, and only seemed interested in ordering more tests. His daughter and son came to visit for many hours each day. During one visit, he was feeling well enough and wanted to sit in the chair to eat lunch instead of sitting in his hospital bed. After eating only half of his meal, Jim told his daughter, "I'm getting this dizzy feeling again." Soon he began to look pale and started to faint. They shared with the nurses that this episode happened right after Jim ate, and asked if it could be something related to his digestion or stomach? "Oh no, we don't think it has anything to do with that," the medical practitioners assured us. Once stabilized, Jim ended up going home with no diagnosis, yet again.

The follow-up visit to the doctor who reviewed all of the findings was futile. Everything looked fine with Jim's heart and his brain. Jim's daughter asked what they should do if Jim were to faint again. The doctor's reply was, "Call 9-1-1." Staring at the doctor as his words hung in the air, Jim's daughter thought, "...And then this circus will happen all over again to result in nothing… *again*?"

Six months later, Jim was once again taken to the ER at a different hospital (at Jim's request). Both are well-known and renowned hospitals. Jim's daughter shared all the information she had about her dad's previous experiences, as did Jim. He was admitted to the hospital, and the next week was a complete nightmare. More of the same tests were done. He was on constant IV and never left alone to sleep for more than 2-3 hours at a time. He told his daughter he felt like the medical staff was torturing him, and he just wanted to be left alone. The sleep deprivation and medications caused him to hallucinate. This made things even worse. The doctor shared that they found nothing from the tests. They suggested exploratory surgery to see what was going on. That revealed plenty. The surgeon shared that Jim had several issues going on in his colon and gut, including that a part of his colon that had become malformed, plus he had diverticulitis and cancer. He died two weeks later.

The story I've shared is a personal one. Jim was my father. He lived a good life in his 89 years, and I am blessed to have had him that long.

Over the next six months, there was a lot to handle. I sat down at one point to review the insurance paperwork from the previous few years. Thankfully, my dad's insurance covered the majority of his medical treatment, because the total cost of care came to over $500,000.

I share the cost to point out the excessive amount of money that went towards less than adequate care (I am being polite) of one patient. I also share the cost for shock value. It certainly shocked the heck out of me and made me sick to realize that this goes on all the time, and we all pay for it through the high cost of our health insurance. If his regular doctors had asked some general questions, I believe they would have been able to get to the bottom of what was going on *years* earlier - (the surgeon shared with me that all of his issues would have been years in the making). If only the hospital had looked slightly south to the gut, rather than solely focusing on his heart... Doctors and specialists with limited time tend to focus on one area of the body, to the detriment of all others. This seems to be commonplace in our current, bottom-line-driven healthcare system, where physician/patient time is dictated by hospital corporations and insurance companies. We need to demand that medical professionals look at the whole person during consultations, that doctors take into account their patient's overall health - aches/pains, activity, diet, life circumstances – everything. Lacking this comprehensive approach, modern medical protocols are resulting in out-of-control costs and a lower quality of life for everyone who comes through the system. I believe that everyone involved with my father's medical madness was just following the 'standard of care' protocol and doing their jobs the way they were told to, not meaning to cause any harm. But unfortunately, the system is not working well, and is falling drastically short in every way.

THE REAL COST OF OUR HEALTHCARE

Could there be a systemic problem with the medical/hospital system that tends to focus primarily on insurance and hospital protocol, and in the process overlooks patients' needs?

The biggest cause of rising healthcare costs is hospitals. This is per the Centers for Medicare & Medicaid Services (CMS), a federal government agency.[56] Nearly half of the *growth* in spending (49%) has been from hospital services.

"The rising cost of healthcare." We hear that statement everywhere. Every year, the standard employee enters into the fun 'open enrollment' time. This is where employees get to review their options for coverage for the upcoming year. We know this process probably won't be pleasant. The process itself is enough to leave a person with health problems. Doesn't it seem that there is a correlation between this strategy of overprescribing medications, tests, and procedures; our funding every person without health insurance; the reckless spending within the medical industry; and the continuous increase in our insurance premiums? For some, medical insurance premiums have reached a level where they can no longer afford the coverage. The rest of us take up the slack, through taxes as well as through paying higher premiums and deductibles.

Every politician has some great speech about his/her mission to fix the situation so that "no American will be without healthcare." Do we really want the government controlling our healthcare system anyway, when their track record isn't all that great when it comes to managing systems and keeping costs down in other areas? That aside, what is really happening behind the scenes that is causing healthcare costs to rise and the system to remain broken? Shouldn't the focus be on fixing the cause and on how costs can be reduced? And, asking Mr. Obvious, shouldn't we all mainly want people to learn to be healthier to begin with? Health education is one great solution.

If our government and the medical industrial complex were so concerned with our health and well-being, why wouldn't there be a campaign to strengthen our immune systems, and to teach people about all of the vital systems throughout the body and how to strengthen them? Why don't we have 30- or even 15-second ads on every channel to educate the general public about some basic preventative measures to reduce the need for expensive pharmaceuticals and medical treatments? Wouldn't essential education about health be a great use of our taxpayer dollars, and one way to reduce healthcare costs? **Answer: There is no money in health. There are billions in healthcare.**

HEALTH OR HEALTHCARE

In the U.S., we have the most expensive healthcare system in the world. Yet, statistically we are not the healthiest culture by a long shot. Perhaps the focus should be more on health than healthcare? We are essentially bought, sold and brainwashed into thinking that there is a pill for every ill, a quick fix, a fast cure; that we don't really have to work at staying healthy; and that we can't prevent anything. We are taught that we are victims of these health challenges that just randomly happened to us, and we're told that we have to go to the doctor for a treatment or pill, then we'll be okay. That's the best we can do.

We now have actors and celebrities selling us medications on a daily basis. It is assumed that they are trustworthy and good role models, and why wouldn't we take their word for it that the stuff is good for us and will help us? Certainly, the high paid celebrity is fully knowledgeable about what they're promoting, knows everything there is to know about drug management, right? We can trust that they've done the research, looked at the data and the evidence, reviewed the risks, and have the background to understand it all. They wouldn't just be promoting some drug or procedure for the money, would they?

Healthcare costs are going up because we are allowing it and, in many cases, encouraging it. At times, it seems that receiving medical care is akin to buying a car, with all the upselling going on. The difference is that rather than being given an *option* of undercoating or fabric protection for your automobile, you are being *told* that you need certain tests and procedures, by someone you are supposed to trust with your life. No pricing or money matters are disclosed or discussed. If our insurance covers it, we don't question anything. The Monopoly money will cover it.

Be your own health advocate and your own sleuth and ask the billing office for a breakdown of the cost of the treatment/procedure/ testing, etc., even if your insurance covers it. We need to start asking these important questions and stop assuming that some magical money out there covers all of it. *We* are covering it in the end.

As long as humans keep getting sick (in this toxic world it's hard not to), and as long as the insurance industry keeps approving the pharmaceutical protocol over any other approach, the modern medical professionals are going to keep making a killing. Yes, I use that word intentionally. Medical error is now one of the top causes of death in the U.S.[57]

The top four causes of death shift from year to year, and vary based on the reporting source, but it's safe to say that these four causes make up more than fifty percent of all deaths in the United States.

1. Heart Disease

2. Cancer (including the top contributors of lung cancer, pancreatic cancer, prostate cancer, colon cancer, and breast cancer)

3. Chronic Lower Respiratory Disease (including asthma and COPD)

4. Accidents (including automobile accidents, medical error of preventable care in hospitals, drug overdoses, and procedures and surgeries gone wrong)

MEDICAL MISHAPS

Estimates conclude that over 1,000 people a day die from human error in hospitals.[58] These people are not dying from the illnesses that caused them to seek hospital care in the first place. They are dying from mishaps that hospital staff could have prevented. What do these errors look like? The sponge left inside the surgical patient, prompting weeks of mysterious, agonizing abdominal pain before the infection overcomes bodily functions. The medication injected into a baby IV at a dose calculated for a 200-pound man. The excruciating infection from contaminated equipment used at the bedside. If you aren't alarmed enough that our country is burying a population the size of Minneapolis every year, due to medical error, hear this- you are paying for it. Hospitals shift the extra cost of errors onto the patient, the taxpayer, and/or the business buying health benefits.

If there are over 1,000 deaths documented per day, what is the number of misdiagnoses or human errors that didn't actually lead to death? Those cases are not always tracked within hospitals, for obvious reasons, but we can assume that the number is higher than that of the deaths. In my own experience, including my father as well as other family and friends, we experienced four (hospital errors and misdiagnoses) in just a two-year period.

INGRID

A good friend of mine, Ingrid, had an unfortunate bicycle accident last year. In the ER, she was examined, x-rayed, and diagnosed with a fractured hip. She was in one of the most respected hospitals in Bellevue, Washington. One would assume that she would have had the best care.

As the aides were transferring her from the gurney to the hospital bed, Ingrid noticed that they were about to handle it incorrectly. She knew the proper protocol for transferring a patient, because she was a registered nurse (RN). She spoke up. The nurse in charge told her everything was fine. Ingrid kept protesting and finally yelled, "No!" They ignored her pleas and proceeded to move her by lifting the sheet on one side to pull while the other aid shoved her right at the point of her fracture. Her foot drifted downward. Ingrid knew right then that her hip was now fully separated.

The series of incidents that happened next is a little unreal. The head nurse came in as Ingrid was screaming in pain. After learning what happened, rather than call in a doctor, the nurse downplayed it. Ingrid asked for another x-ray. The nurse told her, "that isn't necessary, and we don't have an order for that." The nurse did put in an order for narcotics to help her with the pain. Ingrid felt that the narcotics order was more about trying to shut her up than manage her pain. Over the next many hours, she kept insisting on a new x-ray. Her multiple requests went unanswered. She finally threatened to call 9-1-1 to be moved to a different hospital. That stirred things up. An x-ray was ordered. Ingrid insisted on seeing it as well as the initial one taken upon her arrival. She took pictures of both with her phone.

Two hours after being admitted for a basic fracture, now her only option was a full hip replacement. She ended up with soft tissue damage, bleeding in the pelvic cavity, bladder issues, a fully separated hip and off-the-chart swelling. The original need for minor oral pain care turned into needing heavy narcotics (IV and oral).

The aides messed up. No one wanted to admit it. They tried to cover it up. The only reason they even agreed to take another x-ray was because Ingrid threatened to call 9-1-1. She knew that was an option from her extensive experience as an RN (orthopedic nurse, NICU nurse, flight nurse, and more). If no second x-ray had been done, there would have been no evidence of her hospital-caused injury.

The acronym used in the medical industry is PAEs for Preventable Adverse Events. The average cost of a PAE is $50,000–$60,000 per incident.[59] If we base our math on 1,000 mishaps per day (from the stats of the deaths), then we quickly reach over $18 billion in costs in a single year. The true number of non-death incidents is unknown.

Ingrid's story is a real-life example of a PAE. When all was said and done, what should have been a $27,000 matter ended up running over $100,000 that her insurance (or essentially all of us) paid for.

I've learned a lot from Ingrid's experience as well as from others in recent years. There are steps you can take **now** to know your rights and be prepared.

TEN THINGS TO DO BEFORE YOU
OR A LOVED ONE ENDS UP IN THE HOSPITAL:

1. Make prior plans within the family (relations or friends). Who can be your advocate(s) in time of need?

2. Bring an advocate. They are of sound mind when the patient is not.

3. If you feel the care is not as it should be, ask for the house supervisor. If they don't resolve it, ask for the hospital administrator. If that doesn't work, ask for the CEO. Risk management is there to protect the hospital. Don't accept a visit from Risk Management. It is a bit deceiving since they appear to be there to help and assist you. They say all the right things, but their focus is on protecting the hospital's interests.

4. Of utmost importance, if you feel that something is going wrong and if no one is helping, dial 9-1-1. This is a well-kept secret among hospitals. The medics have to come in and assess the situation.

5. Have your advocates take notes when the doctor or other specific caregivers come in. Use your phone to record doctor conversations if you don't have an advocate there during the few minutes that the doctor is in visiting.

6. Ask for your health records before or soon after you leave. You have a right to all of your records—not a redacted version. Look to make sure they give you the entire record.

7. Question all diagnoses and treatment recommendations.

8. Ask questions about everything.

9. Take a photo of the x-ray or whatever comes up on the screen to have a copy that you can reference later.

10. Use your cell phone to call family, friends, or other caregivers if things are going wrong in the hospital during your stay.

BE YOUR OWN ADVOCATE

I used to think that alternative care was another term for hippy-dippy, incense-lighting nonsense. My mother was an RN. My father spent his final career in the medical equipment field. He and his business partner had a successful company that sold and monitored hospital equipment all over the Pacific Northwest. I was raised in a family where doctors and the medical world were well respected and trusted. I never questioned their proposed care and completely trusted what I was advised to do when it came to raising my children. I did have a few eyebrow-raising moments along the way, but I would generally shake off the doubts with thoughts like, "well, they are the experts and what do I know?"

For the past ten years, I have been paying attention, opening my eyes, doing research, asking questions, and diving into the arena of health and wellness. The more I dig, the more I find. Now I believe it is vital for all of us to ask questions, do a little research, get a second (and maybe third) opinion, and consider other options, especially when we or a loved one has a health issue or even during standard preventive care appointments.

Just because you are in the doctor's office, don't feel like you have to do everything they suggest or tell you to do—especially if there is a voice inside your head saying, "That doesn't make sense or sound like a good idea." You have the right to say, "Thank you for that information/suggestion. I'd like to take some time to consider everything before I make my decision." You are their customer. You are paying them for their expertise. You are not under their rule. You have the right to question and to say no (or not right now) to anything they recommend.

It is not fair or ethical for a medical professional to ever belittle or bully a patient into thinking that only they have all the answers. If you are being treated this way, it's time to find another provider who respects your questions, and who you feel you can trust.

There are many competent doctors, nurses and practitioners out there who are saving lives and helping people. They should be applauded. The standard medical system (somewhat handcuffed by the health insurance industry) is seemingly getting in the way of their taking the best care approach with their patients. They need to have more freedom to focus on how healthcare was meant to be, always making the patient's well-being the primary consideration "to do good and to do no harm."

POWER UP — ACTION ITEMS

- Be your own best healthcare advocate.

- Do your own look, learn and discovery work. Be prepared with questions when you consult your physician or healthcare provider.

- Ask many questions. Get second and third opinions when anything seems illogical or if you are in any way uncertain about something.

HIGHER LEVEL

- Prepare **now** - BEFORE you or anyone you care about ends up in the hospital (See ten points above).

CHAPTER 8

THE BEAUTIFUL POWER OF GIVING

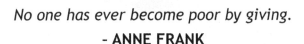

No one has ever become poor by giving.

- ANNE FRANK

We've covered a lot of heavy topics about how we can direct our dollars and decisions to improve our overall health and that of our environment. With the ripple effect, this helps others outside of our own sphere. We can also use our power to help others by giving. Let's change the tone here and look at the *Power of Green* from the giving perspective. There are many ways to give and many people, institutions and causes to give to. The list is as endless as the need. You can use your power very directly for good.

My sister-in-law, Melissa, is a huge inspiration. One Christmas, she shared a special story about anonymous giving. They have a lovely home on a few acres with a barn and horses. A few years ago, we had an unusually long, cold winter. Where they live, propane is commonly used to heat homes. In a conversation with the delivery guy who came out to fill their tank, he mentioned that with the extremely cold weather, people needed more propane than usual. He also mentioned that some people were struggling to keep up.

The thought of other people having trouble staying warm when they could easily afford to stay comfortable did not sit well with my caring sister-in-law. This prompted her to call the propane company to ask if they knew of any families having trouble paying their bill or running low on propane without the financial resources to cover the cost of filling their tank. The woman on the phone said she would ask the driver since they are the ones who go out to the homes, make connections with people, and know some of the personal stories.

Sure enough, the driver knew of an elderly couple who were struggling. Mel offered to cover the cost of the propane they needed. What a relief it must have been for this couple. What a warm (warm all over) feeling this must have generated for everyone involved. It was true giving from the heart. Thanks, Mel, for letting me share your story.

SECRET SQUIRREL GIVING

Another way to use your power is by giving anonymously. There is tremendous positive power for both the giver and receiver in anonymous giving. Perhaps you are out somewhere and overhear a conversation. Understanding and compassion wash over you. Maybe you find a way to slip some cash into an envelope and leave it where you know that person will find it (keep some envelopes in your car). You might ask the waitperson to give it to them after you leave. Or you could just pay their bill.

Perhaps you hear someone speak about a worthy cause, you realize they have a good heart and really want to help people, but you know that they don't have much themselves. You can find a way to anonymously give some money to them with a note encouraging them to share it to help others. This allows them to be a giver too. You are doubling your gift this way. Someone will receive much-needed funds, and you're also *giving* the wonderful and powerful gift of giving.

I first did this many years ago, after listening to someone speak at our church. He wasn't asking for donations of any kind. He (a youth minister, I believe) was sharing a story about an encounter he had with someone less fortunate. I could tell he was a person of integrity and someone with a big heart who really cared about people and wanted to help. He spoke with people all the time who had challenges in life.

I had just received a nice big tax refund, so I went to the bank and had them prepare a cashier's check in his name for 10 percent of my refund amount. I put it in an envelope and slipped it in the drop box slot at the church office directed to him with that little note of "Somewhere there is a need." I'm sure it came as a complete surprise to him. There was no indication as to who it came from or why it was addressed to him in particular. He was probably also perplexed as to why it was an odd amount of money. It was exactly 10 percent of my refund. I never learned what he decided to do with it. But that didn't matter. I did my part. The rest was up to him.

It felt amazing to be able to do that, and I reflect back on it every now and then. This was the start of my secret squirrel giving. You'll never be able to write off any of these as charitable contributions on your tax returns (I know that's crossing some of your minds). But what you will receive in return will be immeasurable—more than you can imagine. I've never shared my stories of secret giving with anyone. And I wasn't ever planning to. I only share this one now in hopes that you and others reading this will follow suit, or that it will spark ideas of your own. Once you have your radar out, things will surface. You will know when you are in the right place and time to help someone.

You will likely never see the look on their faces or receive any direct gratitude or thanks. But that is the point. The powerful positive energy created within you and within the recipient, and the reverb out from that, is magnified when it is done this way. Give it a try, and you will see for yourself. They will send out an energy of thanks, and you will feel it.

When you sense that internal tap or tug—your instinct—you need to listen to that and consider acting on it. Find a way to anonymously give. It will be more powerful than you can imagine. The people who are in need and receive your help will feel the light of your intention. You will benefit from the pure and true giving, where you know, and God (or your greater order defined) knows. The Universe knows. This elevates your purpose and your being. This can be part of your legacy.

It does not have to be a huge sum. It may not even be money. Give what you can. Do what you can. This will improve your health and overall well-being. And it will spill out the same all around you.

POWER OF EDUCATION

There is a small school, high in the hills in the rural countryside of the Dominican Republic, where children are smiling and happy to be educated every day. They are cared for by their teachers and are the hope for the future of their families. Most have parents with little or no education, who work in low-wage jobs and are barely able to make ends meet for themselves and their families. This is a pattern. Most see no alternative. They know enough to understand, however, that if their children can be educated, they may have more opportunities in life.

I had the opportunity to see these children and their school while vacationing in the Dominican Republic. I took a long trek on a rickety tour bus one day, along with others, far from our large and lavish resort on the tourist beaches of Punta Cana. The little schoolhouse was near the highest altitude point on our tour. It was surrounded by beautiful greenery, quiet land, lovely birds and flowers. Its primitive beauty made it seem like a land from long ago. Our tour guide was a nice man who had been very jovial and enthusiastic about sharing the history of his country and people along the tour. As we pulled up to the schoolhouse, his tone changed. He was very serious about what he shared next.

In a very contemplative voice, he said, "You will notice there are older children outside the schoolhouse who will approach when you step off the bus. They will beg and say anything that has worked in the past to communicate they are desperate and need your help. Please do not give them any money. This only encourages them to continue to come back every day. They keep coming back and have no incentive to go to school. Later they will not try to get work and help themselves and their families if people continue to hand them money. Or the work they are able to get with little or no education will not provide enough. This does not help them. It hurts them. And it sets a bad example for the younger children who see this and may decide to follow that path."

He went on to explain that the school was trying to help children in the region to break the cycle of poverty. He expressed how fortunate he was to have a good job that allowed him to care for his family. He had seen enough and was experienced and educated enough to know that the only way his people could prosper was if the next generations got a good start with continued education on that path.

Wow. This was the first time I had ever been on a tour in a foreign country where we were actually encouraged to withhold our money. It really made me think. The tour guide was right. It showed how much he truly cared for his people and his country.

We exited the bus and were escorted to the small building. The youngest children were in this classroom. Those who were a little older were outside waiting for the buses to come around.

The little room was crammed with tables and children. The bright-faced children were well behaved, positive and wide-eyed. They looked alive, well, hopeful, and happy to be in the classroom.

The older children outside who were begging for money had a completely different look on their faces and energy about them. They looked very worn and old for their ages, even though they were probably only a few years older. It was as if they had already carved out their profession and had accepted that they were destined for a life of begging.

There were more children inside the classroom than there were outside, so it seemed like the tour guide's effort to educate tourists was working. This was a lesson for all of us. We had never considered that throwing money at a cause cannot only be the wrong approach, but it can often be damaging. The damage can result in encouraging the very thing you are trying to turn around.

Our guide stated that if we felt we had to give them something, we should come back and bring pencils or school supplies—something that would encourage them to stay in school.

People learn from watching other people. Those children see us as rich. And compared to their world, we certainly are. We have an opportunity to set an example for them. Instead of just throwing money in their direction, we can demonstrate that education is the most important thing. With an education, they not only help themselves, but they can also help other family members who are not educated. And they become good role models for their siblings, others around them, and for future generations.

What can be learned from this? Throwing money at a cause is not always the best solution. We must look at the true, desired result and how our money energy—the power of our green—can be best used to achieve it.

PHILANTHROPY — A FAMILY AFFAIR

There is perhaps no better way to leave this earth than with a well-thought-out plan for the final act of your power of green. This is your last opportunity—your last message to the world and to those you love. What do you want that message to be?

A will is important for many reasons, no matter what your net worth is. If you don't have one or if it is out of date, I recommend you get on it right away—even if that means typing up your own one-page document for now. You absolutely can do that and have it witnessed or notarized. If you do not have any sort of will, you could be leaving your money to the government or creating a mess for family members to deal with. I would guess that is not what you want your final act to be. Of course, there are many nuances, and working with a professional is the best approach when creating a will.

Family and loved ones are probably the main focus of your legacy giving. In addition, think about the opportunity you have at this point and consider additional approaches.

In her wonderful book *Give to Live*, author Arlene Cogen covers a myriad of ways people can use their *Power of Green* to leave a legacy after they are gone as well as while they are still living. Over the years, Arlene has helped individuals and families understand the giving process in ways they never imagined. Perhaps my favorite example from the book was that of Marco and Maria.

Marco came from a hard-working family of little means. Over the years, with Maria's support, he built the family wealth to an impressive level. He and his wife strongly believed in giving back, and they wanted their children and grandchildren to continue the tradition.

Among Arlene's creative options for a portion of their legacy was for them to establish a donor-advised fund for the purpose of family giving. They specified that $120,000 of this fund was to be used now rather than after their passing, thus seeding the tradition.

Marco and Maria wanted each family member to be engaged, so each person in the family was given a specific amount to donate to a nonprofit organization of their choice—each could give to a cause they cared about. Half of the designated amount ($60,000) would be used for these individual gifts. Split among twelve family members, they would each have $5,000 to contribute to their individual cause. With the remaining $60,000, the family would decide collectively which one or two organizations they would support with a major gift to make a more significant impact.

Marco and Maria decided to introduce their plan at Thanksgiving, as they knew the whole family would be there. Each member would receive their portion. At Christmas, they would come back and share what organization they had given to and why. Can you imagine a Christmas where instead of the day revolving around opening gifts that you don't really need; you talk about the difference you're making in the world? That is what happened to this family, and now it has become an annual tradition that's brought them all closer together. Later, Marco and Maria shared that it was the best Christmas they ever had.

Even the small amount you may spend on a gift for each family member can be turned into something that encourages good, positive use of money and allows people to explore *The Power of Green*. Think outside the box. Start your legacy now.

TEACH TO TRANSFORM

Another approach to giving can be in the form of teaching others. Over the last ten years, Linda Bolton and her husband Dale built a very successful distribution business in Canada. The success of their business has allowed them to travel, which is one of their passions.

On a trip to Africa, they visited an orphanage in Kenya. The children and people touched their hearts. They felt compelled to help. They reflected on how their life together was comfortable and in order. They had plenty of food to eat, clothing, comfortable housing and the ability to travel. They were educated and savvy enough to have built their business to a successful level where it not only enhanced their lives, but also had a positive impact on many others.

Their thought was to create a plan and put a structure in place that would make a meaningful difference in the lives of those they had met at the orphanage, as well as for the surrounding communities. The idea was to create a model that would not only benefit the people who were currently there but would also create forward energy to continue helping for generations to come.

They put their business knowledge to work to determine what the the people really needed. Rather than throwing money at the matter and hoping that would make a difference, they put together a structure that would not only help nourish and empower the children, it would also produce actual income for the local communities while providing invaluable training and education to pass forward.

In 2008, they created and opened Thrive (thriveforgood.org) in western Kenya. Their tagline is *Planting hope. Harvesting change.* The approach is multi-faceted, focusing on four key themes—organic gardening, nutrition, natural medicine, and income generation.

Thrive brings in people from rural communities to educate and train them in all four themes. At the same time, they are trained to be trainers, so they bring their knowledge back to other people in their communities. In Africa, there are many challenges to farming. By teaching the locals how to address these unique constraints, the program helps the extreme poor lift themselves to the next rung of development, creating a brighter future for themselves and the children in their communities.

Linda describes one big concept that she and her husband learned along this path: The cycle of poverty is never going to end if people keep giving handouts... the same message I heard from the guide on my Dominican Republic trip. Teaching people to take care of themselves is the best way to provide lasting support.

Dale and Linda have created something that will likely be felt for generations to come. What a legacy. We can applaud them for their generosity—not only giving their money, but also their time, and most of all, their hearts. I am sure the people of western Kenya are grateful. And what they have done creates a ripple effect.

This is the model we should all pay attention to. Teach people how to support themselves within their communities and have them educate others to do the same. Create a structure that can be passed down from generation to generation, where a viable income can be earned, and health and self-worth will be enhanced. In addition to the practical benefits that those who are taught a skill will gain, they also gain a sense of fulfillment from being positive role models guiding and supporting their loved ones and those in their community. The Thrive model is caring, nurturing, logical and sustainable. And it is a wonderful and positive example of the *Power of Green.*

There is no reason this model cannot be replicated on our continent to meet the needs of our struggling communities— by individuals and by our government. If the government's goal is truly to help people, help the economy, and help the country, let's encourage them to structure programs that educate and train people to help themselves.

Our model for the basics of food, health and wellness seems to be based on a reliance and dependency structure. This creates a slow, downhill slide and sets people up for failure. A focus on real-food nutrition leads to a stronger immune system, which leads to fewer health issues, which leads to lower healthcare costs for everyone. Having some simple education about how to nourish our bodies and minds to avoid illness and disease, and how to support our overall well-being, will reduce the costs of healthy food and healthcare. By empowering people to care for themselves well and encouraging less reliance, we can change the course of our country and be a shining example for others. It starts with each one of us.

POWER UP – ACTION ITEMS

- Try some secret squirrel giving. Start small and see how it goes. You may want to build from there.
- Be cautious about giving handouts of money to people. If it discourages them from getting the help they need, this is not truly helping. Try a different approach.
- Update or create your will *now*. This can be simple to start.

HIGHER LEVEL

- Use a professional to help you prepare/update your will.
- Encourage your loved ones to continue the giving practice.
- Teach and guide others to pay it forward.

CHAPTER 9

OUR PLANET. OUR HOME.

*The nature of our future depends
on the future of our nature.*
- AUTHOR UNKNOWN

Everything we do, every way we use our *Power of Green* affects our home planet. Picture living in a world where we were only allowed one house per family, and that house would be passed on to all future generations of the family. If that were the case, wouldn't we do everything possible to take the best care of it? Wouldn't we feel a sense of responsibility to keep it in the best shape possible?

Given that thought, I'd like to state here that it is not *the* planet, it is *our* planet. It is most likely the only one we will ever know in our lifetime. We are passing it along to future generations of our own families, our friends, and their families. We should take good care of it. The choices we make with our dollars today will be felt for all future generations to come. Let's see how one individual is showing the world how working with nature can bring a piece of the earth back to life and leave a lasting impression.

HOW LAND LIFE CAN BE RESTORED

Picture tumbleweeds blowing around the dry, uninhabited areas of Texas. In 1969, one man had a mission and took a journey. He set out to locate the most desolate, unhealthy land he could find to show that, with the proper attention, it could be restored. Born into poverty in Ohio, David Bamberger got his love, respect, and understanding of the natural world from his mother. He started out selling vacuum cleaners to support himself, and eventually met and partnered with Bill Church of Church's Fried Chicken in San Antonio, Texas. Together they built the company to over 1,600 stores. They eventually sold the company. Being a man of integrity and generosity, he set out to do some good. He decided to put his love of nature to the task.

He wanted to show that by working with Mother Nature, instead of against her, land could not only be restored, but also brought to a point of rich health. After some searching in the hill country of Texas, he came across a very worn, dry, and nearly lifeless land that no one wanted. It was the worst piece of land he could find. It was a wasteland. It was perfect.

There was very little life on the 3,300-acre parcel of land. There was no surface water or live creeks. The wildlife was minimal at best. There was little to no grass to feed the creatures. What was surviving was weak and frail. The first order of business was to try to find where the water was and why it was not coming to the surface. Seven water wells were drilled 500 feet deep. Not a drop of water was found.

The top 125 feet was dry and parched. They finally found an aquifer, but it was bone dry. He knew that at one point in time, water did flow there. He set out to see how he could make that happen again. Certain limestone can be like coral in the ocean. It has holes and caverns that will hold water underground when conditions are healthy. The land was flush with limestone, but no water.

They did some surveying of the land and made an assessment of what they could do to encourage the natural water to return to the aquifer. Water builds in an aquifer over time from rainfall, but it won't if nature doesn't have anything moving it downward. They removed certain trees on the hillside where this dead aquifer was located and replaced them with native grass. The root systems of the grass would provide the simple magic that was needed. With the native grass there, the root systems go deep. The rainwater is pulled down and delivered to the aquifer. Once filled, the water has to escape.

After two and a half years, the first spring came to life. As time passed, more sprang up. Streams, rivers and ponds developed, and life blossomed. Nature just did its thing. Birds, animals and all forms of wildlife returned, and are now thriving on the land. What was once a dried-up wasteland is now a well-known nature preserve. Now, the water from the thriving land (in addition to the wildlife on the now 5,500-acre preserve) supports nearby families and even sends water down to the city of Austin. People come from all over to visit and marvel over the beauty of **Selah Bamberger Ranch Reserve**.[60] Books have been written about the place. Thousands of photographs have been taken and published capturing some of the most beautiful images of nature in that area of the country. David Bamberger has since donated the land to a foundation so it will live on after he is gone. It seems he surely achieved, and likely surpassed, his initial goal.

Billions of dollars are spent by the government (our money) on dams, reservoirs and pipelines. Is that necessary? For some of these human-made water features, maybe, for our modern way of living. But all of them? There is definitely an ongoing cost of building these obstructions, both monetary and otherwise. Are the powers that be overlooking some fairly simple and inexpensive approaches that would actually be much sounder in the long run? Certainly, working with nature rather than against her is generally going to be best. Why not let nature do most of the work in the end? She wants to and her work is free! This is the *Power of Green* at its finest.

Let's encourage our decision-makers to look at what others have already done, which has yielded stellar results. Mr. Bamberger's project is just one of countless thousands of prime examples all over the world of individuals and organizations working with nature to achieve amazing results. If there is an alternative to massive and costly human-made projects, that should be considered first.

Politicians love to promote huge projects that will create thousands of jobs for their community and improve the local economy. It all sounds so good when they speak of this "brighter-future-for-all" vision. Who doesn't want that? What they generally omit and don't want us to look at is the true cost and/or the downside. How many millions of our tax dollars are pouring into this? Is that the only way? What is the environmental cost that we will all have to pay down the road? There will be consequences when we go against nature. Humans will never outsmart her in the long term.

Perhaps if our so-called leaders would put forth a little time and effort in researching some proven, successful ways to work with nature, they could come up with alternate solutions that could still create jobs, improve the local economies, and actually improve the health of the environment at the same time. We have some brilliant minds on this planet. Put some of them in charge of coming up with long-term solutions, rather than the politicians and corporations who are currently at the helm, only looking at the short-term gains for themselves. Working in harmony with nature and each other, corporations can still profit. Jobs can still be created. Politicians can still look good to the people – probably even better, when they wake up and live more in alignment with the laws of our natural home.

What if all of this could be done at a fraction of the cost, too? Can you imagine if that were the focus? Imagine your tax dollars going toward something that was good for all, and for generations to come.

Selah is said to mean to stop, pause, look around, and reflect on everything you see. Mr. Bamberger certainly did just that and has subsequently created a wonderful place on our planet where others can do the same. He set the example of taking something that was barren, dry, and neglected; he nurtured it back to life and set it free for all to enjoy, for all time. We can absolutely do more to pause, look around, and reflect on what we see, and then assess what we can do (or encourage others to do) for the best and brightest outcome.

BACK TO EDEN

Another amazing example of simple ways we can work with Mother Nature or have her do the work for us, I discovered at a small farm just on the other side of Puget Sound in my home state of Washington. If you take the ferry from Seattle across the water to Bainbridge Island, and then keep driving northwest, you'll come upon a wonderful place that will warm your heart and blow your mind. Back to Eden Farm is the creation of Paul Gautschi (gow-chi).[61] Paul moved his family up to the Olympic Peninsula in the late 1970s. He had been gardening since he was a child. Growing up, his family farmed in the traditional ways - tilling, plowing, weeding, watering. It was Gautschi's intention to use what he knew to homestead their land and grow their own food. They drilled a well. But the well only produced a half gallon a minute, which he knew was never going to be enough.

The summer of 1979 was exceptionally warm. The grass was all brown. There was beautiful sunshine, but how on earth would they be able to grow food with no water? He pondered the situation. Looking around at the lush, surrounding woods got him thinking. How are all of these huge trees, bushes, and plants continuing to grow and thrive in this exceptionally dry season? So, he went into the woods. He looked at the ground, got down on his hands and knees, and dug in. The top layer was leaves and twigs and matter from the surrounding trees and vegetation—underneath was the surprise. It was beautiful, rich, healthy soil. At that moment, he had a realization. Nature knows what it's doing!

He had local arborists haul over their woodchips. The woodchips recreated the groundcover of the forest. When the rains came, the downpour turned the nutrients from the wood into liquid nutrition for the soil underneath. The soil transformed, becoming fertile, moist and highly nutritious, building up the biology, the microbes and the good bacteria in order for Eden's crops to thrive.

There were years of experimenting on the farm. Paul learned that all he needed to do was put down four to six inches of woodchips and let nature do the rest. Each year got better and better. It was a dream. And now, Gautschi's soil looks like beautiful black compost under the chips. He has tried it all: straw, grass clippings, rocks, leaves and animal manure; but he always goes back to woodchips. Woodchips are not bark or shavings or sawdust. The chips are parts of branches, leaves and trunks that have been chipped by local arborist services, which the tree trimmers need to get rid of, so they will drop the chips almost anywhere for free.

Basically, the Back to Eden gardening method is a way to garden using nature's intended growing environment. It is all about recreating the environment in which plants already thrive. Nature blossoms by using the resources it has. The groundcover is both protection and insulation. That, and some occasional rain, are all that's needed.

For more than 30 years now, Paul Gautschi has been growing fruit trees and the most incredible varieties of vegetable plants that you can ever imagine. He never fertilizes, and he lets nature (rain and groundcover) do the hydrating. Peach trees, apple trees, blueberries, raspberries, every vegetable you can imagine, herbs, flowers and more flourish in Paul's garden. He grows it all. His fruits and vegetables are beautiful and delicious, I can attest.

In agriculture, there is a lot to deal with... soil preparation, fertilization, irrigation, weed control, pest issues, crop rotation, PH issues, and more. None of those problems exist when nature is allowed to be herself and thrive naturally. There are many approaches to working with nature versus fighting against her. Some ways work better in one area than another. Some are better for small scale and some for large scale gardening ventures. The point is that we humans are absolutely smart enough and have the resources to figure out ways to grow our food so that it nourishes the land as well as ourselves and our animals, without doing any harm.

If you think about it, nowhere in nature do you see exposed dirt. The soil is always protected. The ground is a living organism. Humans have skin, birds have feathers, animals have fur, fish have scales, bugs have shells… and the land has groundcover. We all have our protection. When we start tilling the soil and scraping off nature's protection, the soil starts to dry out and nutrients die. When you take the cover off, it dies. Where do we see this? In our own backyard. The Midwest is almost desert-like now. Decades ago, it had the richest soil in the nation. Now it calls for millions of gallons of water every day and an obnoxious number of chemicals to grow anything. This is not sustainable and is slowly diseasing and killing us.

I'm not sharing this story with the thought that you are going to rush out and want to start growing your own fruits and vegetables, though that would be fabulous. The point here is that there are alternative ways to grow food and plants without harmful chemicals. IT IS POSSIBLE. Nature's way is always better for human health and our planet's health than synthetic chemical processes that kill and destroy. Growing crops naturally does not only work on a small scale. Large scale organic farming can also work given the opportunity, whether it be some form of what Paul has created or another. There are amazing things happening out there with farmers all across the U.S. and in other countries who are standing their ground and not giving in to the pressures or bullying tactics of the companies who push the chemicals and anti-nature approaches. We all need to take this seriously and do what we can as consumers to shift the tide.

We've covered a lot of ground, discussing consumerism, clothing, trash, food, farming, health matters, hospitals, devices and how we can make a positive difference for ourselves, others and our planet by maintaining a higher level of awareness and using our *Power of Green* to change our trajectory. Our world today is vastly different than it was just a century ago. Some of our modern changes have been incredible and for the better. Perhaps with other changes, people should have taken more time to think them through.

Is there anywhere in the world that seems to be on the best path? Actually, yes. There are a few places on the planet that are considered by many to be the healthiest and happiest. We may not want to leave the creature comforts of our modern world for these spots on the globe, but we can certainly learn from them.

BLUE ZONES

Live long and prosper. This is a phrase that many know from Mr. Spock on Star Trek, but it can also be traced back to a traditional Jewish blessing. The sentiment is the same—wishing people well through a good, long life. What does a good, long life mean? Mention living to age 100 and some will say they don't want to live that long. Perhaps they relate it to the thought of being a burden (financially and otherwise) to others, being unable to do the things they love, being restricted in movement, confined to walkers/wheelchairs, being in pain and suffering, being bedridden, left alone, ignored, or any number of unpleasant things that we experience or witness with our aging parents, grandparents, or others these days in the U.S.

Who wants to live a long life under those circumstances? Is that how it has to be? We all certainly want to live a healthy life feeling good, moving freely, with good brain function and the ability to be active until our last days.

Natural Geographic decided to devote time and resources to see where in the world people were living the best quality, longest lives. Enter Dan Buettner, author and *National Geographic* fellow.[62] He and a team traveled around the world to see what they could find. What they uncovered was extraordinary.

They discovered five regions/communities across the globe where people consistently lived not only the longest, but lived healthy, active, high-quality lives through their final years. These areas they refer to as blue zones.

- Okinawa, Japan
- Ikaria, Greece
- Sardinia, Italy
- Nicoya, Costa Rica
- Loma Linda, California

These five regions across the world have the very lowest rates of cancer, heart disease and diabetes, (the top disablers and killers of people in the U.S., responsible for much of our healthcare expenses). Americans spend billions of dollars on protocols that fail. What is going on in these blue zone communities that blows our sorry stats off the map?

What is most amazing about Buettner's research is his discovery that, despite the fact that the locations are spread across the planet and completely independent of one another, all five zones share commonalities of habits and living styles.

Natural Movement - The people don't have an exercise regime, gyms, or fitness plan. They move naturally with the activities they do each day – mainly outdoors (walking, biking, gardening, daily activity).

Sense of Belonging – They are not isolated from one another. They live in communities where they interact on a daily basis. They feel a sense of faith and purpose in life.

Plant Slant - They eat a predominantly plant-based diet (90-95%). The food is native to the area in which they live. Food is often grown by the people and shared. Vegetables, beans, and seeds are the staples. They don't eat food shipped in from other countries.

80% practice - They stop eating when they feel 80% full (delayed communication between stomach and brain). They eat from smaller dinner plates.

Wine @ 5 - They enjoy a little wine or drink with their main meal. Yes, yay. But in small quantities.

Family - They have a family-first attitude. They care for, stay connected with, and support one another.

Pause - They take time each day to down-shift/de-stress with prayer, meditation, stretching, gathering with family, and friends, or a variety of methods to create a pause, and quiet the mind.

Elder Honor - One thing that is unique to and universal across all of the blue zones is that the elderly are honored. No matter the age, people respect their elders. The younger generations appreciate and learn from their knowledge and wisdom. They are valued and treated well. Who wouldn't want to grow old under those circumstances?

Dan and many on the team speak around the world about their journey and discoveries. They've partnered with AARP to roll out blue zone's lifestyle practices in select towns around the United States. One of their first projects was in Albert Lea, Minnesota. They worked for months to improve the lifestyle practices of its citizens by mimicking the commonalities of the blue zones they researched. Healthcare costs were reduced by 40% in less than a year and there were many other positive results. **This should be front-page news and studied by everyone and anyone involved in improving healthcare in America.**

The most notable part about the people in the blue zones is that they are less likely to get sick as they age. They are not just surviving – they are thriving. Instead of the deterioration process that we consider to be normal aging, their longevity is a continuance of the healthy lifestyle they've enjoyed for their entire lives. They don't live to the age of 70 or 80, then start a slow, miserable mental and physical decline; they have freedom of movement with their bodies, clear thought, and communication, and an actual enjoyment of life until the very end (usually into their 90s or 100s). AND, they have the respect, appreciation and attention of their family members and community. Can you imagine having that to look forward to in your elder years? What a lovely way to finish a life.

From 2017, when *National Geographic* published the blue zones findings, until now (and with Dan and his team speaking around the world), there are ample opportunities to learn more about this incredible yet simple approach to living a better life for the remaining years we have. Take time to study, ponder, and adopt practices however you can. Be the change you want to see in the world. Live long and prosper.

POWER UP — ACTION ITEMS

- Encourage our community leaders and politicians to look at all sides before making decisions that will have long-term effects on our health, our tax dollars and our planet.

- Consider what you can do (and encourage others in your community to do) to put some of the blue zones habits into practice to work toward a healthier and happier existence and duration of life.

HIGHER LEVEL

- Study or visit blue zones if you have the opportunity.

IN CLOSING

There is so much more to be said about each of the subjects covered in this book, and so many other topics that were not covered. The objective of *The Power of Green* is to create an awareness in relation to everything around us, so we can view the world with a better understanding of what is really going on. We can make changes and adjustments within our power to slow the ship down. We can send a message to the captain and the crew that the passengers are not going to sit by and do nothing and watch as the destruction happens, as the ship goes down, lives are lost, and people suffer.

Take a look at where we are headed with the health of our planet. How long can we continue at our current pace? What can we do as individual inhabitants to leave the world a little better than how it is right now?

Look around as you go about your day—as you make decisions and spend your money. Practice intentional spending. Pay attention. Be observant, learn, ask questions, and be curious. Don't assume. Use your intuition. Listen to that little voice in your head asking questions and wondering. How are you using your power today? Send the message. Direct it toward what you want to make better.

Use the power of your voice. Sometimes it needs to be strong. But sometimes subtle is good. You can cause a ripple effect with one slight comment to a stranger or within a conversation with a friend or coworker. Create awareness where there is none. When people become aware, change is possible.

PURPOSE

Have you determined your core purpose in life? I know that's a biggie. Whether you already know it or are on the journey to discovery, somewhere inside of you probably lies a yearning to do something positive that will help others. Are you waiting for some set life benchmark to start? Time is a-wasting! Opportunities are being missed. You can start right this minute by making a commitment to use your *Power of Green* wisely and purposefully every day. Everything you do adds up.

There is an intersection between awareness and our fast track through life. Sit in that space every once in a while. Pause and reset.

I like material things as much as the next person. And I'm not saying don't spend your money. Just spend it consciously. There are better ways to send out our money energy. We don't need a massive quantity of possessions or the latest and greatest of everything to make us happy. There will always be something newer and better out there. It's a losing game. Don't play. Be grateful for what you have every day. Every day- live, love, laugh, hug and share. Hugs are good. Left shoulder to left shoulder creates a heart connection.

Be bold and unafraid to question the status quo. Be mindful. Voice-vote. Plant seeds everywhere you go. Be the example. Grow your green and use it for the betterment of all and for this big beautiful rock we live on.

A big heart hug and thanks for reading my book. Please share it with others... the hug and the book!

ARE YOU WILLING TO SHARE YOUR STORIES TO INSPIRE OTHERS?

In writing *The Power of Green*, I've used my own power of green (time, money, effort, and energy). I share points meant to inform, inspire, and encourage you to open your eyes and take charge. Use your own power to improve your life as well as the lives of others. You will make your own discoveries and begin to notice things that you never noticed before, but which were there all along.

I encourage you to share your personal stories of discovery and insight as you put your strategies into practice. I would love to hear your stories, so that I can then share them with others for their learning and benefit. Take a moment to think about your discoveries. What has impacted you and what adjustments did you make or what actions did you take along the way?

Please send your stories to me along with your permission to share them with the world. Yours may be chosen for future print. We can all learn from one another.

I look forward to hearing from you!

Amy O'Brien

thepowerofgreen@byamyo.com

HOW TO USE YOUR POWER

There is no time like the present!
You can make positive changes to impact
yourself and your family starting now.
Big or small steps, you'll create your own
ripple effect to help others.
The world needs you!

To receive helpful tips on any of the Power Up Action Items, email:

thepowerofgreen@byamyo.com

In your email, list the specific topic(s) you would like to focus on.
You'll receive information in one or more of the following forms:

- Suggestions/Guidelines
- Checklist of tasks
- Suggested video to watch
- Deeper-dive information for added learning

All the best with your continued journey!

ENDNOTES

1   Schueler, Gerald J., "The Sensitive Dependence on Initial Conditions" The Wanderling. http://the-wanderling.com/initial_conditions.html.

2   MacVean, Mary, "For many people, gathering possessions is just the stuff of life" March 21, 2014. Los Angeles Times. https://www.latimes.com/health/la-xpm-2014-mar-21-la -he-keeping-stuff-20140322-story.html.

3   Statista Research Department, "Toy Industry – Statistics & Facts" August 21, 2018. Statista. https://www.statista.com/topics/1108/toy-industry/.

4   BeWell, "A clean, well-lighted place" Stanford. https://bewell.stanford.edu/a-clean-well-lighted-place/.

5   Gordon, Lisa Kaplan, "The Link Between Clutter and Depression" houselogic by Realtors. 2019 https://www.houselogic.com/organize-maintain/cleaning-decluttering/clutter-depression/.Citation

6   Drew, Deborah and Yehounme, Genevieve, "The Apparel Industry's Environmental Impact in 6 Graphics" July 5, 2017. World Resources Institute. https://www.wri.org/blog/2017/07/apparel-industrys-environmental-impact-6-graphics.

7   LeBlanc, Rick "Textile and Garment Recycling Facts and Figures" April 27, 2019. Nationwide. https://www.thebalancesmb.com/textile-recycling-facts-and-figures-2878122.

8   Rouse, Margaret. "Definition Greenwashing" September 2017. Whatis.com. https://whatis.techtarget.com/definition/greenwashing.

9   Books, Simon "15 Countries with The Cheapest Labor" January 22, 2017. Money. https://www.therichest.com/world-money/15-countries-with-the-cheapest-labor/.

10 Hardash Productions "Fashion Factories Undercover (Documentary)" August 6, 2016. Real Stories. https://www.youtube.com/watch?v=HHw4HEzzsyc.

11 Amir "Top Countries with Largest Textile Industry" October 29, 2015. Country Ranker. http://www.countryranker.com/top-countries-with-largest-textile-industry/.

12 Wikipedia "Charles J. Moore - Great Pacific Garbage Patch" https://en.wikipedia.org/wiki/Charles_J._Moore.

13 The Swim "The Great Pacific Garbage Patch Is Not What You Think It Is" December 3, 2018. https://www.youtube.com/watch?v=6HBtl4sHTqU.

14 Visser, Nick "The Ocean is filling up with Plastic Smog" IMPACT May 24, 2017 https://www.huffpost.com/entry/plastic-pollution-oceans_n_59104e54e4b0d5d9049dc664.

15 Marine Bio "Marine Biodiversity" February 16, 2019 https://marinebio.org/conservation/marine-conservation-biology/biodiversity/

16 Our World Ocean https://oceanservice.noaa.gov/

17 Sciortino, D.G. "Starving Seabirds Found with Full Bellies but Not with Food" June 25, 2018 https://animalchannel.co/sea-birds-starving-bellies-full-plastic/

18 Earth Day "Fact Sheet: Single Use Plastics" March 29, 2018 https://www.earthday.org/2018/03/29/fact-sheet-single-use-plastics/

19 Ewing, Gabrielle "A Brief History of How Plastic Has Changed Our World" National Geographic. https://video.nationalgeographic.com/video/magazine/planet-or-plastic/00000163-50c4-d011-ab67-75c52e020000.

20 Toxicology Data Network "Methyl acrylonitrile" 2001. NLM-Toxnet. https://toxnet.nlm.nih.gov/cgi-bin/sis/search/a?dbs+hsdb:@term+@DOCNO+5613.

21 World Atlas "How Is Plastic Made?" August 1, 2017. https://www.worldatlas.com/articles/how-is-plastic-made.html.

22 O'Connor, Mary Catherine "Only 14% of plastics are recycled -can tech innovation tackle the rest?" February 22, 2017. The Guardian. https://www.theguardian.com/sustainable-business/2017/feb/22/plastics-recycling-trash-chemicals-styrofoam-packaging.

23 Mosbergen, Dominique "Here's Why America is Dumping Its Trash in Poorer Countries" March 9, 2019 Mother Jones https://www.motherjones.com/environment/2019/03/heres-why-america-is-dumping-its-trash-in-poorer-countries/.

24 The Ocean Cleanup "How It All Began" 2013. https://theoceancleanup.com/milestones/how-it-all-began/.

25 Slat, Boyan "How the oceans can clean themselves" October 24, 2012. TEDx Talks. https://www.youtube.com/watch?v=ROW9F-c0kIQ.

26 Slat, Boyan "How we will rid the oceans of plastic" May 2017. The Ocean Cleanup. https://www.youtube.com/watch?v=du5d5PUrH0I.

27 https://www.merriam-webster.com/dictionary/food.

28 Cafasso, Jacquelyn "How Many Cells Are in the Human Body?" July 16, 2018. Healthline. https://www.healthline.com/health/number-of-cells-in-body.

29 Frank, Alex – Denison University. "We Broke Down the 19 Ingredients in McDonald's French Fries to Find Out What We're Eating" Spoon University. https://spoonuniversity.com/lifestyle/mcdonald-french-fries-ingredients.

30 Schaefer, Anna "The Potential Dangers of TBHQ" July 16, 2019. Healthline. https://www.healthline.com/health/food-nutrition/potential-tbhq-dangers.

31   Diet.com "High-Protein Diet"
     https://www.diet.com/g/highprotein-diet?get=highprotein-diet.

32   Campbell, T. Colin. *The China Study*. Dallas, Texas: BenBella Books, 2006.   ³⁵ ³⁶ ³⁷ ³⁸ ³⁹

33   Mills, Dr. Milton MD. "Humans Designed To Be Vegan? What About Canine Teeth?"
     July 23, 2018. Plant Based Science London. https://youtu.be/xdJ0RTOUI98.

34   https://dictionary.cambridge.org/us/dictionary/english/oligopoly.

35   Kramer, Anna. "These 10 companies make a lot of the food we buy." December 10,
     2014. OXFAM. https://www.oxfamamerica.org/explore/stories/these-10-companies-
     make-a-lot-of-the-food-we-buy-heres-how-we-made-them-better/.

36   CBC Marketplace. "Here's what's in your bottled water" April 6, 2018. CBC News.
     https://www.youtube.com/watch?v=I75qa0kTeY4.

37   Common, David and Szeto, Eric. "Microplastics found in 93% of bottled water tested in
     global study. April 6, 2018. CBC News.
     https://www.cbc.ca/news/technology/bottled-water-microplastics-1.4575045.

38   CBC Marketplace. "Here's what's in your bottled water" April 6, 2018. CBC News.
     https://www.youtube.com/watch?v=I75qa0kTeY4.

39   wocomo DOCS. "Poisoned Fields – Glyphosate, the underrated risk?" January 25, 2016.
     wocomo.

     https://www.youtube.com/watch?v=XDyI10Z8aH0.

     Trustwell " Roundup Lawsuit" 2019. Trustwell Law Group.
     https://www.trustwelllaw.com/environmental/roundup/
     lawsuit?utm_source=bing-ads&utm_medium=paid-search&utm_
     campaign=roundup&msclkid=f81222033b91101866a57f7b0cb6b154&utm_
     term=glyphosate%20cancer&utm_content=Glyphosate%20Cancer%20%7C%20Exact.

     #F24Debate. "Ticking Time Bomb? Cancer Lawsuits Mount for Monsanto
     Over Glyphosate" May 14, 2019. France 24 English. https://www.youtube.com/
     watch?v=RLeF2RBAi5I&feature=youtu.be.

40   wocomo DOCS. "Poisoned Fields – Glyphosate, the underrated risk?" January 25, 2016.
     wocomo. https://www.youtube.com/watch?v=XDyI10Z8aH0.

41   Bunge, Jacob. "Health Agency Says Widely Used Herbicide Likely Carcinogenic" March
     20, 2015. The Wall Street Journal. https://www.wsj.com/articles/health-agency-says
     -widely-used-herbicide-likely-carcinogenic-1426885547.

42   GMOs Revealed "Buyer's Remorse: Bayer Stock Plummets over News of Monsanto's
     Court Ruling: August 14, 2018. http://www.gmosrevealed.com/buyers-remorse-bayer
     -stock-plummets-over-news-of-monsantos-court-ruling/?gmo-bayer-stock.

     Goldberg, Max. "Interview with Dewayne Lee Johnson – Monsanto" April 10, 2019.
     Livingmaxwell.com. https://www.youtube.com/watch?v=3hsS6ieL-zo.

43   "Edwin Hardeman v. Monsanto Company | Federal MDL Bellwether Trial" Baum
      Hedlund Aristei Goldman, PC.

      https://www.baumhedlundlaw.com/edwin-hardeman-v-monsanto/.

      Levin, Sam. "The family that took on Monsanto: "They should've been with us in the
      chemo ward" April 2019. The Guardian. https://www.theguardian.com/business/2019/
      apr/10/edwin-hardeman-monsanto-trial-interview.

44   "Pilliod v. Monsanto Company | California Roundup JCCP" Baum Hedlund Aristei
      Goldman, PC. https://www.baumhedlundlaw.com/pilliod-v-monsanto-trial/.

      Randazzo, Sara. "Roudup Verdict Cut to $87 Million From $2 Billion" July 25, 2019. The
      Wall Street Journal. https://www.wsj.com/articles/roundup-verdict-cut-from-2-billion-
      to-86-7-million-11564104196.

45   "NOAA forecasts very large 'dead zone' for Gulf of Mexico" June 12, 2019. NOAA.
      https://www.noaa.gov/media-release/noaa-forecasts-very-large-dead-zone-for-gulf-of-
      mexico.

      "Lousiana: Downstream Dead zone" May 17, 2009. Blue Legacy International.
      https://www.youtube.com/watch?v=jr2AnVxr7C4.

46   Rabalais, Nancy. "The 'dead zone' of the Gulf of Mexico | Nancy Rabalais" May 20, 2018.
      TED. https://www.youtube.com/watch?v=5zWmdHmJMd0.

47   EPA. "Basics of Green Chemistry" Environmental Protection Agency.
      www.epa.gov/greenchemistry/basics-green-chemistry.

48   Resources for You (Radiation Emitting Products). "Putting Television Radiation in
      Perspective" March 12, 2018. FDA.https://www.fda.gov/radiation-emitting-products/
      resources-you-radiation-emitting-products/television-radiation.

49   Health Physics. *The Radiation Safety Journal.* February 2008. Volume 88, Number 2.
      Health Physics Society by Lippincott Williams & Wilkins. Hagerstown MD.
      https://www.nrc.gov/docs/ML0504/ML050400427.pdf.

50   Cirino, Erica. "Should You Be Worried About EMF Exposure?" October 23, 2018.
      Healthline. https://www.healthline.com/health/emf

51   An Independent Information Resource of Peer-Reviewed Research into the Impacts
      of Electromagnetic Fields on Humans and Our Environment. "EMFS + Male Fertility"
      EMF Research. https://www.emfresearch.com.

52   Del Sol Beaulieu, Josh. "Take Back Your Power" August 23, 2018.
      https://www.takebackyourpower.net.

53   Blumenthal. "Senate Commerce Hearing, Blumenthal Raises Concerns on 5G Wireless
      Potential Health Risk" February 9, 2019. RFSAFE. https://youtu.be/hsil3VQE5K4.

54   "Optical fiber" April 17, 2015. Wikipedia. https://en.wikipedia.org/wiki/Opticalfiber.

55   Adams, Kelly M., Lindell, Karen C., Kohlmeier, Martin and Zeisel, Steven H. "Status of nutrition education in medical schools" June 2008. PMC-US National Library of Medicine National Institutes of Health. https://www.ncbi.nlm.nih.gov/pmc/articles/PMC2430660/.

"An Academic Conflict: Pharma's Increasing Influence on Medical Education" April 9, 2014. Case Western Reserve University School of Law https://www.youtube.com/watch?v=GG5Q2SGkqLY.

56   Miller, Harold D. "Redesigning Health Care from The Bottom Up Instead of from the Top Down" Center for Healthcare Quality & Payment Reform. www.CHQPR.org. http://www.chqpr.org/downloads/HaroldMiller_AffordabilitySummit_09-27-17.pdf.

57   Marcus, Mary Brophy. "The top 10 leading causes of death in the U.S." June 30, 2016. CBS News. https://www.cbsnews.com/news/the-leading-causes-of-death-in-the-us/.

58   McCann, Erin. "Deaths by medical mistakes hit records" July 18, 2014. Healthcare IT News. https://www.healthcareitnews.com/news/deaths-by-medical-mistakes-hit-records.

59   Bernazzani, Sophia. "Tallying the High Cost of Preventable Harm" October 5, 2015. Costs of Care. https://costsofcare.org/tallying-the-high-cost-of-preventable-harm/.

60   "50 Years Ago, This Was a Wasteland. He Changed Everything" April 24, 2017. National Geographic. Short Film Showcase. https://youtu.be/ZSPkcpGmflE and www.Bambergerranch.org.

61   "How to Grow a Vegetable Garden – Back to Eden Organic Gardening Film" December 2, 2016. Dana & Sarah Films. https://www.backtoedenfilm.com/ and https://www.youtube.com/watch?v=6rPPUmStKQ4.

62   "5 'Blue Zones' Where the World's Healthiest People Live" April 6, 2017. National Geographic. https://www.nationalgeographic.com/books/features/5-blue-zones-where-the-worlds-healthiest-people-live/.

Buettner, Dan, "How to live to be 100+" April 17, 2013. TED-Ed. https://www.youtube.com/watch?v=ff40YiMmVkU.

Buettner, Dan. *The Blue Zones Solution*. National Geographic; reprint edition May 30, 2017.

Made in the USA
Coppell, TX
24 March 2020

17559183R10079